FREEZER MEALS COOKBOOK

45 + Tasty Make Ahead Freezer Recipes for Meaty Dishes

(My Best Freezer Meal Recipes and Tips for Freezer Meals)

Michael Freeman

Published by Alex Howard

© Michael Freeman

All Rights Reserved

Freezer Meals Cookbook: 45 + Tasty Make Ahead Freezer Recipes for Meaty Dishes (My Best Freezer Meal Recipes and Tips for Freezer Meals)

ISBN 978-1-990169-52-6

All rights reserved. No part of this guide may be reproduced in any form without permission in writing from the publisher except in the case of brief quotations embodied in critical articles or reviews.

Legal & Disclaimer

The information contained in this book is not designed to replace or take the place of any form of medicine or professional medical advice. The information in this book has been provided for educational and entertainment purposes only.

The information contained in this book has been compiled from sources deemed reliable, and it is accurate to the best of the Author's knowledge; however, the Author cannot guarantee its accuracy and validity and cannot be held liable for any errors or omissions. Changes are periodically made to this book. You must consult your doctor or get professional medical advice before using any of the suggested remedies, techniques, or information in this book.

Table of contents

Part 1 1

Introduction 2

Bagel Bombs 4

Veggie Mac & Cheese 7

Oatmeal Cups 10

Chicken & Black Bean Enchiladas 12

Chicken Nuggets 15

Hamburgers 17

Fish Fingers 19

Beef & Ale Pie 21

Sweet Potato & Black Bean Empanadas 24

Lasagne 27

Chocolate Banana Loaf Cake 31

Chicken Tikka Masala 34

Cheesy Vegetable Bakes 37

Pancakes 40

Sweet Potato Breakfast Burritos 43

Garlic & Lime Chicken Kebabs 47

Potato Gnocchi 49

Chicken Pot Stickers 52

Lentil Chilli 54

Winter Vegetable Soup 56

'Monkey Tails' 59

Raspberry Cheesecake Squares 61

Mint Brownies 64

Cottage Pie 67

Shrimp Stir Fry 70

Cheese & Ham Stuffed Chicken 73

Pepperoni Pizza Puffs 76

Vegetarian Moussaka 79

Creamy Chicken Pesto Pasta 83

Sweet Potato, Spinach & Chickpea Curry 86

Part 2 89

Introduction 90

Delicious Freezer Recipes 92

Recipes Included In This Book 92

Freezer Recipes 94

Baked Chicken Nuggets 94

Beef And Noodle Casserole 96

Cheesy Veggie Chowder 97

Creamy Chicken Casserole 98

Burrito Bake 99

Cheesy Greens Roll Ups 101

Chicken, Ham And Cheese Casserole 102

Cheesy Ham And Potatoes	103
Make Ahead Mac And Cheese	104
Classic Pot Roast	105
Chicken Parmigiana Bake	106
Make Ahead Mongolian Beef	107
Breakfast Burritos	108
Beef And Mushrooms	109
All-American Casserole	110
Veggie And Mozzarella Farfalle	111
Homemade Frozen Pizza	113
Easy Bake Chicken Pot Pie	114
Creamy Chicken With Salsa	116
Baked Spaghetti	117
Buttermilk Pancakes	118
Creamy Parmesan Chicken Penne	119
Baked Pork Chops	121
Turkey Loaf	122
Lemon Garlic Chicken	124
Homemade Freezer Meal Recipes	125
1) Pork Tenderloin With Seasoned Rub	125
2) Lasagna Rolls	127
3) Spaghetti And Meatballs In Tomato-Basil Sauce	129
4) Vegetable Lover's Chicken Soup	132

5) Mini Chicken Burgers With Herbs 134
6) Baked Mac & Cheese 136
7) Turkey Tetrazzini 138
8) Blueberry Pumpkin Baked French Toast 141
9) Baked Beef Ravioli 143
10) Mocha Brownies 145
11) Pumpkin Chili 147
12) Chipotle Chicken Chili 149
13) Firecracker Asian Salmon 151
14) Whole Wheat Pumpkin Pancakes 153
15) Slow Cooker Marinara Sauce 155
16) Stuffed Poblano Peppers 156
17) Homemade Pizza Sauce 159
18) White Chicken Pizza 161
19) Homemade Freezer Jam 164
20) White Bean, Sage, And Sausage Soup 165
21) Honey-Garlic Chicken Kabob Marinade 167
22) Broccoli-Cheese Chowder 169
23) Roasted Lemon-Garlic Chicken With Veggies 171
24) Mini Mushroom And Sausage Quiches 173
25) Curried Corn Bisque 175
26) Iberian-Style Sausage & Chicken Ragù 177
27) Sausage Gumbo 179

28) Jamaican Beef Patties 181

29) Squash, Chickpea & Red Lentil Stew 184

30) Chile & Beer Braised Brisket 186

Part 1

Introduction

The Freezer Meals Cookbook

We can definitely all relate to not wanting to cook. Even if it's something we love, there are some days when you just need a good meal and put your feet up. So, having a bunch of delicious home-cooked meals just happily stored away in your freezer could be the answer to all of those problems.

But what exactly do we mean when we say 'make-ahead freezer meals'? How will this actually save you time if you still have to make the meals yourself? Well, there are really 2 ways you can go about this:

1) Make extra portions of ingredients when you do have the time to cook, and freeze the leftovers

2) be SUPER organised and set aside a day to do a tonne of meal prep. You can probably easily make and freeze 30 portions in a day – and then eat super easy for a month!

If you fancy having on demand Creamy Chicken Pesto Pasta, Beef & Ale Pie, Fish Fingers or Mac & Cheese, but without having all the additives and generally not good stuff that comes with ready-meals, then this is for you!

For Chicken Nuggets, Breakfast Burritos, Chocolate & Banana Loaf Cake and Sweet Potato, Chickpea & Spinach Curry, just turn the page and let's get cooking!

Bagel Bombs

Yep, these are delicious bagels that absolutely EXPLODE with yummy stuff. There are few combinations are more authentic than breakfast's very own 'ham, egg and cheese'. I know it's not just me who knows for a fact that melted cheese is the most superior state of cheese! Of course, these bagels can be made ahead, you can double, triple, quadruple the batch – the sky is the limit(!) – and frozen for a quick bagel hit whenever the need arises!

Makes: **8-12**

Preparation time: 80 minutes + at least an hour rising time

Ingredients:

For the bombs:

- 8 oz. shredded cheese
- 5 eggs
- 5 oz. ham
- 1 tablespoon honey
- Sesame seeds to top
- Poppy seeds to top
- Dried onion to top
- Dried garlic to top

- Pinch of salt
- Pinch of pepper

For the bagel dough:

- 4 ½ teaspoons yeast
- 3 ½ cups bread flour
- 1 ½ oz. sugar
- Pinch of salt

Serving suggestion:

Well, what is fun way to get out of that breakfast, rut, right? And so, any good breakfast is deserving of a fresh cup of coffee to accompany it!

1) To make the bagel dough, first mix the yeast and sugar into 1 ½ cups of warm water. Set it aside for 3 minutes. Mix 2 cups of the flour with a good pinch of salt, and then stir the yeast mixture in. Then, mix in the remaining flour.

2) Flour a surface and knead the dough for 5 minutes, until firm. Place the ball of dough in a greased bowl and then cover with cling wrap. Leave the bowl so that the dough can rise for an hour or more, until the dough has doubled in size. Then, punch the dough down and divide it into 8-12 balls.

3) Scramble the eggs by whisking them up, and seasoning well with salt and pepper, before adding into a pan. Use a spatula to keep moving the eggs around, so that as soon as they stick, they are moved, to create the 'scrambling'.

4) Preheat the oven to 425F and line a baking tray with parchment paper.

5) Flatten each ball of dough into a disk using your hand. Divide the scrambled egg between each piece, and then sprinkle ham and cheese onto each one too.

6) Pull the sides of the dough up and over the filling, sealing the edges with a little water, if necessary, to keep it closed tightly.

7) Add 12 cups of water into a pan and stir in the honey when it has come to the boil. Place the bagels in, for just a minute each, turning them halfway through to ensure even boiling.

8) Place the boiled bagels onto the baking tray, with the sealed side down. Sprinkle on the toppings you have chosen, and then bake for 25-30 minutes.

9) Enjoy some warm, and then wrap the remaining bagel bombs in cling wrap and freeze for future use.

10) To cook from frozen: Unwrap the bagel and then wrap it in a paper towel. Microwave for just over a minute on high so that the bagel warms through and the inside gets all gooey and delicious again!

Tips: If you want to cut out a lot of the time needed to make this, then try using pre-made pizza dough. Do everything exactly the same, and by the end result, you'll not even notice the difference!

Put whatever you like in the filling, of course! For those of us with a sweet tooth, here is a FANTASTIC idea! Make cinnamon and raisin bagels, by adding cinnamon and raisins into the dough when mixing. Fill with spiced honey apple filling, or, for the big kid inside of us, banana and Nutella!

Veggie Mac & Cheese

Mac & Cheese is without a doubt one of the all-time family favourite dishes. Of course, we pretend we've made it 'as a treat for the kids', but there is not one of us who doesn't do a little jump for joy at begin able to indulge in this ultimate comfort food. The only problem is that traditionally, Mac & Cheese is not the most healthy of all dinners, in fact, there's rarely a vegetable in sight! Well, this version is packed full of hidden veggies. It retains its delicious 'Mac & Cheesiness', but now it doesn't have to be just a 'treat' – it's a healthy midweek dinner!

Serves: 6-8

Preparation time: **50 minutes**

Ingredients:

    12 oz. whole wheat macaroni
- 6 oz. broccoli
- 6 oz. cauliflower
- 6 oz. spinach
- 6 oz. carrots
- 2 cups skimmed milk
- 2 cups cheddar
- 2 tablespoons dried parmesan

- 2 tablespoons butter
- 1 onion
- 1 cup vegetable broth
- ¼ cup flour
- ¼ cup breadcrumbs
- Pinch of salt
- Pinch of pepper

Serving suggestion:

Well… we don't want to go too overboard with the healthiness, do we? Come on, treat yourself to some garlic bread alongside your mac & cheese. Check out the tips section for how to make your own version, freezable too, of course!

1) Set a large pan of water on to boil and add a good pinch of salt.

2) Chop the broccoli and cauliflower up into florets, and peel and slice up the carrot.

3) Once the pan is simmering, add in the macaroni, broccoli, carrot and cauliflower.

4) Once the pasta is 'al dente', after 7-10 minutes, most likely, remove the pan from the heat and strain the water out.

5) In a pan, begin to heat the butter. Peel and dice the onion and begin softening it.

6) Then, add the flour and leave to cook for a minute before then whisking in the milk and vegetable broth.

7) Bring the mixture to the boil, and then reduce the heat and allow the sauce to thicken for 5 minutes and stir in a pinch of salt and pepper.

8) Shred the cheddar and stir it into the sauce until smooth.

9) Then, stir the macaroni and vegetable mix into the sauce and mix everything well until well combined. Pour into an ovenproof dish.

10) Sprinkle the breadcrumbs and parmesan on top.

11) To cook immediately: Have the oven preheated to 375F and bake the dish for 15-20 minutes, before broiling for 2-3 minutes to crisp up the topping.

To freeze: Cover the dish with foil or cling wrap and keep in the freezer. When ready to cook, bake at 375F for 30-40 minutes and then broil for a few minutes to get the crispy topping too.

Tips: Of course, this doesn't have to be e vegetarian meal just because it's full of veggies! Add in some bacon, ham or chicken to bulk it out even more. Make sure that the meat is cooked first before baking.

If you're already in full swing in 'freezer mode' and you have frozen veg, then that's absolutely fine to use too!

Oatmeal Cups

So, why, you may ask, would you want to freeze oatmeal? It's not exactly difficult to make on a daily basis, is it? Well, let me tell you why! It's obviously cheaper to buy oats and customise your own interesting oatmeal, than it is to buy packages of the exciting stuff! Also, do you ever have the problem that I do, where you are really craving a certain fruit, but 'tis not the season? Well, freezing fruit preserves it for months on end! So, if it's mid-winter but you just have to have some left over raspberries, there's no problem if you cleverly froze some for later!

Makes: **24**

Preparation time: **10 minutes**

Ingredients:

- 3 cups oats
- 3 cups almond milk
- ¼ cup brown sugar
- Pinch of salt

Toppings of your choice – try raspberry, macadamias and white chocolate chips, blueberries and ginger, apple, walnut and spices, or almonds and crystallised ginger?

Serving suggestion

I know it would be somewhat an infusion of cuisines (but we're not against that, are we?) but serving this with garlic & coriander naan bread is fantastic.

1) Into a saucepan, add the oats, brown sugar, almond milk and 3 cups of water. Bring the mixture to the boil.

2) Reduce the pan down to a simmer for 2-3 minutes.

3) Divide the mixture into muffin tins, and then add on the toppings of your choice.

4) To freeze: Wrap the muffin tins in cling wrap and freeze. Warm in the microwave for 1-2 minutes, and then add in extra milk, if desired.

Tips: Use the milk to add extra flavour in. For example, try a 'tropical oatmeal', using pineapple and coconut milk.

Use 1-3 cups per serving. So, making 24 will get you at least 8 breakfasts for 10 minutes of labour – awesome, right?!

Chicken & Black Bean Enchiladas

Alright, let's start by clearing up one of the burning questions in life – what makes an enchilada not a burrito or a chimichanga (or vice versa)? I'm going to be honest – I have found so many different answers over the years and I'm not really sure which is correct, but, as far as I can figure it out, here is the answer; enchiladas are usually made with corn tortillas, whilst burritos are made with the flour kind. Enchiladas are smothered in sauce and baked, whereas burritos are just wrapped in the tortilla and so are easy to eat on the go! And, a chimichanga is a deep fried burrito (yes, that does sound fantastic but they don't fare very well in the freezer so we have to work with what we've got!)

Serves: 4

Preparation time: **35 minutes**

Ingredients:

- 16 oz. skinless, boneless chicken
- 15 oz. canned black beans
- 8 corn tortillas
- 8 oz. canned tomatoes
- 4 oz. green chillies
- 2 garlic cloves

- 2 tablespoons flour
- 2 teaspoons chilli
- 1 ½ cups shredded cheese
- 1 onion
- 1 cup chicken broth
- 1 teaspoon cumin
- 1 teaspoon paprika
- ½ teaspoon oregano
- 1/3 cup tomato salsa
- ¼ cup oil
- Pinch of salt
- Pinch of pepper

Serving suggestion:

Prepare some rice and a fresh cilantro and chilli salad and you're good to go!

1) Begin heating a little of the oil in a pan. Peel and dice the onion and garlic and begin to soften them in the pan.

2) Add the chicken into the pan and allow it to begin cooking for 5 minutes or so.

3) Then, stir in the cumin, paprika, 1 teaspoon of chilli and the oregano, coating the chicken well.

4) Next, add in the canned beans and salsa. Dice the chillies and stir them in too.

5) Leave the sauce simmering and thickening for 5 minutes. Then, remove from the heat.

6) Heat the remaining oil in a separate pan, and then stir in the flour and second teaspoon of chilli. Then, stir in the canned tomatoes and chicken broth. Leave simmering for 10 minutes to thicken, and season with salt and pepper.

7) Pour half of the tomato sauce into the bottom of an over-safe dish.

8) Divide the chicken mixture equally between the tortillas, lining it up in the centre so that they can be folded up easily.

9) Line the tortillas up in the baking dish and pour on the remaining tomato sauce.

10) Sprinkle of the shredded cheese.

11) To freeze: Cover the dish with foil or cling wrap and freeze. Before cooking, store in the refrigerator for 24 hours to thaw, and then bake at 400F for 15 minutes.

Tips: As always, taste and adjust the spice mixes to your liking.

For an easy vegetarian dinner, just skip out the chicken and fill with loads of yummy veggies. You can even make both in one dish. Simply use vegetable broth instead of the chicken, obviously. Prepare the chicken in a separate pan and add extra veggies into the bean mix. Then, just add the chicken to some enchiladas – and remember which ones they were!

Chicken Nuggets

Time to level with you – I am NOT a fan of frozen food. I really hate the idea of paying more to buy food that is higher (usually) in fat, salt, sugar and calories, is not fresh, and still requires that you do some work anyway! I know that every now and again, it's fantastic to have something quick and easy to prepare for dinner after a long day of work, but I don't think that that's quite right. But we DO need something to just shove in the oven and not have to think about, right? So, why not make ahead, when you do have the time, and freeze to serve at your convenience? Chicken nuggets are a freezer favourite, I know, and so here is a quick and easy version you can make yourself!

Makes: **24**

Preparation time: **40 minutes**

Ingredients:

     16 oz. ground chicken
- 1 cup breadcrumbs
- ¼ cup dried parmesan
- Pinch of salt

Serving suggestion:

A healthier version of the classic chicken nuggets and chips would be to make these, and fresh potato wedges, which literally just involved chopping a potato into wedges and baking them – super easy!

1) Mix together the breadcrumbs and parmesan with a pinch of salt.

2) Separately, mix a little salt into the ground chicken.

3) Measure about a tablespoonful of the chicken mixture at a time and roll it in the breadcrumb mixture.

4) Toss each 'nugget' gently between your hands to flatten it slightly and create that traditional 'nugget' shape.

5) Cover in the crumbs again to ensure a good coating.

6) Line a baking tray with parchment paper and lay the chicken nuggets on there. Cover the top with another layer of parchment paper and freeze.

7) To cook from frozen: Preheat the oven to 375F and bake the nuggets for 25-30 minutes. If you're not cooking from frozen, take about 5 minutes off of the cooking time.

Tips: If possible, use chicken that has been twice or three times ground. This makes for a better texture.

Add paprika or other herbs and spices to the breadcrumb mix for added flavour.

Hamburgers

I don't think I need to convince you that making your own hamburger patties is infinitely superior to buying them pre-made. This way you know EXACTLY what is going into them, and you can adjust the flavourings to make it EXACTLY the way you like it. You can make a tonne of extras and have them frozen for whenever the need for a burger arises – and it will!

Makes: **6**

Preparation time: **20 minutes**

Ingredients:

- 32 oz. ground beef
- 4 teaspoons paprika
- 3 teaspoons black pepper
- 1 teaspoon brown sugar
- 1 teaspoon garlic powder
- 1 teaspoon onion powder
- Pinch of salt

Serving suggestion:

How can I tell you how to make a burger? I don't have that right, but I'm going to do it anyway! Find a soft bun, toast it slightly, melt cheese on top of the patty, grill up some bacon, slice tomato, add lettuce, douse in ketchup and just enjoy the whole amazing experience!

1) Combine the black pepper, garlic powder, brown sugar, onion powder and a pinch of salt.

2) Mix ¾ of the mixture into the ground beef with your hands.

3) Then, shape it into 6 burger patties in your hands.

4) Sprinkle a little of the leftover spice mix on both sides of the patty.

5) To freeze: Layer the patties on top of each other to store, with a layer of parchment paper in between each one. Allow them to thaw for 2 hours before you want to cook them, and then grill to your desired level of doneness.

Tips: You know what's awesome about ground beef patties without egg in them?? – You can cook them as little as you want!! Now of course, I don't want raw burgers, but there is nothing more disappointing than an overcooked burger!

These, like many burgers, are just perfect for barbecuing - yay! Just allow them to thaw and then slap 'em on!

Fish Fingers

Another absolute freezer filling classic is fish fingers. I know for sure that there are days when your kids come home, clamouring that they're starving hungry, and, if you're anything like my mother was, she would offer me 'fruit' or 'a yoghurt', which was absolutely NOT what we wanted! Sometimes, she was give in and let us have an early dinner, and, although she was very good at healthy home cooking, sometimes we did have 'freezer meals'. Fish fingers are a huge favourite, so here's how to make and freeze your own!

Makes: **12**

Preparation time: **15 minutes**

Ingredients:

    24 oz. white fish
- 2 tablespoons yellow cornmeal
- 1 ¼ cups breadcrumbs
- 1 egg
- 1 teaspoon mild curry powder
- 1/3 cup desiccated coconut
- Pinch of salt

Serving suggestion:

I know it's not exactly gourmet, but I have such a love affair with fish finger wraps! I'm actually a big kid and I love ketchup in them too. For a more grown-up version, use tartar sauce in the wrap instead.

1) Slice the fish into sticks, about 3 inches long and less than an inch thick.

2) In a bowl, mix together the bread crumbs, curry powder, coconut, cornmeal and a pinch of salt.

3) Separate the egg and whisk the white with a tablespoon of water.

4) Dip each piece of fish first into the egg white and then dip into the bread crumb mixture and coat it all over on all sides.

5) To freeze: Place the fish fingers on a baking tray and freeze for 2 hours until they're frozen through. Then, to save on space, you can simply remove them from the tray and keep them in a Ziploc bag until you're ready to use them. Bake for 15 minutes and enjoy!

Tips: You can replicate this process and make... wait for it ... mozzarella sticks! Do it exactly the same, just use mozzarella instead of fish, simples!

Save the yolk and use it to go towards making your own mayonnaise to dip your fish fingers in to avoid any wastage!

Beef & Ale Pie

This is one of those recipes that by rights should have the word 'proper' at the beginning of the title. With all the amazing things that we can do with food nowadays – make 'free-from' versions, or fusion foods, or even creating dished that look sweet but taste savoury, as delicious as they may be, sometimes we just need a little trip back to our roots, for some 'proper' food. If you were born and raised in the UK, for example, then a traditional food that should be defined as 'proper' is the humble savoury pie. And this is not just any pie, my friends, this is 'proper' beef & ale pie. This is 'pub grub', and boy is it good!

Serves: 6

Preparation time: **30 minutes**

Ingredients:
For the pastry:

    23 oz. plain flour
- 8 3/4 oz. butter
- Pinch of salt

For the filling:

- 35 oz. braising steak
- 13 ½ oz. beef stock
- 10 fl oz. dark ale
- 7 oz. bacon lardons
- 7 oz. mushrooms
- 4 carrots
- 4 tablespoons plain flour
- 2 onions
- 2 tablespoons vegetable oil
- 1 bunch fresh thyme
- Pinch of salt
- Pinch of pepper

Serving suggestion:

The way to eat pie is with mash, I cannot compromise on that! With beef gravy too, of course, and some token vegetables!

1) Preheat the oven to 285F.

2) Heat the vegetable oil in a large pan. Chop the braising steak into pieces yourself, if necessary, and begin browning the outside of the meat. Once it's browned, remove the meat and any juices from the pan, and set aside for later use.

3) Peel and dice the onions and the carrots and add them into the pan with the meat. Cook everything together on a low heat for about 5 minutes.

4) Sprinkle in the 4 tablespoons of flour for the filling and stir until it's mixed in.

5) Next, pour in the beef stock and the ale, and add back in the braising steak and its juices.

6) Season the stew with salt and pepper and add in the thyme.

7) Cover the pan with a lid and place the stew into the oven to continue cooking for 2 hours, until you have amazingly tender meat!

8) Fry up the bacon bits until crispy.

9) Then, add the mushrooms into the pan with the bacon and fry for 3-5 minutes until tender and golden. Then, set the pan aside.

10) When the stew is cooked, stir in the bacon and garlic. Then, refrigerate the stew overnight.

11) Crumb the flour and butter together with your fingers. Add in a good pinch of salt, and then pour in up to 6 ¾ fl oz. of ice cold water to bring the dough together.

12) Knead the pastry, and then loosely wrap it in cling wrap. Refrigerate for an hour.

13) Set aside a third of the pastry. Roll the two third part of the pastry out into a circle and place it into the pie dish you'll be using, pressing it into the edges with your fingers.

14) Add the beef filling into the pie, until it is a heaped pile up to just above the rim of the pie dish.

15) Roll out the remaining one third of pastry into a circle that will cover the top of the pie and overhang the edges a little. Trim the edge, and crimp it with your fingers. Now, you can store it in the freezer until ready to serve!

16) To cook from frozen: Beat an egg and brush the pastry with it. Then, bake for 50 minutes, or more, if necessary, at 285F.

Tips: It's not necessary to refrigerate the stew overnight, of course, but your pastry is likely to turn out better if the filling is cold when its added inside.

Although the sauce of the stew will be full of flavour, and it's great to have a meaty pie, do take care not to add too much of it into the pie, or you may end up with soggy pastry. You can serve the left out gravy warmed with the pie when its ready though!

Sweet Potato & Black Bean Empanadas

Honestly, I'll sneak sweet potato in wherever I can! I am fully converted to the sweet potato train – any recipe uses a regular potato, you can bet your bottom dollar I'm going to replace it with sweet potato if at all possible! The sweet potato works delightfully inside these neat little empanadas, which make a great snack or quick lunch. Make a batch of these, freeze 'em, and use them when the need for sweet potato arises over the next few weeks!

Makes: **10**

Preparation time: 30 minutes + 1 hour of refrigeration

Ingredients:
For the pastry:

    2 cups plain flour
- 1 egg
- 1 tablespoon cider vinegar

- 1/3 cup vegetable oil
- Pinch of salt

For the filling:

    2 sweet potatoes
- 2 spring onions
- 2 tablespoons chopped, fresh cilantro
- 1 chilli
- 1 egg
- 1 cup canned black beans
- 1 tablespoon cumin seeds
- 1 teaspoon chilli powder
- Pinch of salt

Serving suggestion:

Obviously, from frozen you'll heat these, so they'll be all warm with their delicious, crumbly pastry. For lunch, whip yourself up a chunky tomato salsa too, to serve alongside the empanada.

1) Mix the flour and a pinch of salt together,

2) Stir together the oil, vinegar, egg and ¼ of a cup of iced water.

3) Add the oil mixture slowly into the flour, incorporating everything together until it's moist. Then, turn the dough out onto a lightly floured surface and knead it until it's nice and soft.

4) Shape the dough into a ball, and wrap it in cling wrap, before refrigerating for an hour.

5) Set the sweet potatoes into a pan of boiling water, for about 10 minutes until tender. Then, run them under cold water to remove the skin, and mash them, roughly, leaving a few chunks is okay.

6) Grill your chilli until the skin is blacked. Then, when it's cool enough, peel off the skin, remove the skin and dice up the flesh. Chop the green onions too.

7) Place the cumin seeds into a pan for about a minute, to become fragrant. Then, grind up into a powder.

8) Mix the ground cumin together with the mashed sweet potato, chopped chilli, green onions, black beans, chilli powder, fresh cilantro and a pinch of salt.

9) Divide the dough into 10 equally sized pieces, and roll each piece out into a circle, roughly 5 inches wide.

10) Separate the egg and lightly beat the white.

11) Spoon 3 tablespoons of the sweet potato mixture into the centre of each dough circle. Use the egg white around the edges to seal the empanada shut by folding it in half over itself, covering in the filling. Cut 3 diagonal slits on the top of each, for the steam to escape from when cooking.

12) Then, place the empanadas into a freezer safe container, adding a sheet of parchment paper between layers and freeze until needed!

13) To cook from frozen: Lightly beat an egg and brush it over the top of the pastry. Have the oven preheated to 400F and bake for 15-20 minutes, until you can see that the pastry is a nice golden brown colour.

Tips: If you want to change up the spices and herbs in the filling, then go ahead and do that, making it to your taste. We just happen to have a vague Mexican theme going on right now.

You could make mini versions and serve as a party snack!

Lasagne

Lasagne, I have to say, sadly has been abused. Why do I say that? Because it is really one of the ultimate 'freezer meals'. Of course, freezer meals are not wrong. What I don't like is that it has become a meal that, although a classic, is rarely made in the home anymore. Lasagne comes in that metal container and goes straight in the oven, with no cooking involved. Don't get me wrong, I know that some days, having something to just whack in the oven is a great thing, but why not prepare the lasagne on a day when you do have the time, so that you'll still have the satisfaction of knowing that you're eating a home-cooked meal. I recommend making 4 or 5 if you can (and if you have the freezer space!) so that you'll have a lasagne to hand at all times!

Serves: 6-8

Preparation time: **120 minutes**

Ingredients:

- 35 oz. ground beef
- 33 fl oz. milk
- 14 oz. chopped tomatoes
- 8 ¾ oz. lasagne sheets

- 6 ¼ oz. butter
- 4 ¼ fl oz. dry white wine
- 4 ¼ oz. plain flour
- 3 ½ oz. grated parmesan
- 2 eggs
- 2 teaspoons grated nutmeg
- 1 celery stick
- 1 carrot
- 1 red onion
- 1 sprig fresh rosemary
- 1 bay leaf
- ¾ cup mozzarella
- ¾ oz. dried porcini mushrooms
- Pinch of salt
- Pinch of pepper

Serving suggestion:

As long as you're not worried about the carbs, the way to serve lasagne is with garlic bread and potato wedges! Sweet potato wedges are a good way to reduce the carbs, though.

1) Roughly chop the porcini and then soak them in hot water for 8-10 minutes.

2) Begin melting 3 ¾ oz. of the butter in a large pan.

3) Meanwhile, peel and dice the onion, carrot and celery.

4) Once the butter is foaming, add the onion, carrot and celery into the pan, along with the fresh rosemary and a good pinch of salt and pepper. Drain the porcini and stir them in too.

5) Add in the ground beef, stirring it around until it's browned, and then pour in the white wine and canned tomatoes.

6) Bring the mixture to the boil, and then reduce the heat down to low and cover the pot. Cook for an hour with the lid on, and

then remove the lid to continue cooking for another 30 minutes. Then, taste and season again with salt and pepper, if need be.

7) In a separate pan, add the milk and the bay leaf. Bring it to the simmer and then remove from the heat.

8) Melt the butter in a saucepan, and then whisk in the flour and the hot milk mixture.

9) Whisk until smooth, removing the bay leaf, and then leave it cooking for 10-15 minutes until it's really thickened up.

10) Remove the bay leaf, and then season with the nutmeg, salt and pepper to taste.

11) Separate the eggs and stir in the 2 yolks along with the parmesan cheese. Remove from the heat.

12) Set a pan of lightly salted water on to boil. Then, plunge each lasagne sheet into the boiling water, for just 10-20 seconds, to soften slightly. Once out of the boiling water, immediately put the sheets into a bowl of iced water, to stop them from sticking together.

13) Into your freezer and oven safe lasagne dish, add a layer of lasagne sheets to cover the whole bottom. Add on a layer of the beef ragu, and then a layer of the white sauce.

14) Cover with another layer of lasagne sheets and keep repeating the process until you're out of either pasta, ragu, or white sauce (hopefully it'll happen at roughly the same point!)

15) Slice the mozzarella and lay it all over the top of the lasagne. Then, cover the dish with foil and freeze until ready to use.

16) To cook from frozen: Have the oven preheated to 285F and bake the lasagne for 40-50 minutes until everything is bubbling and the cheese is melted and browning.

Tips: Easily make this vegetarian by using quorn mince in place of the beef, of by just filling that ragu up with all the vegetables you can lay your hands on!

I believe that there is never a thing as too much cheese! So, if you're a really cheesy person, you can add other cheese on top too. If you're one for strong flavour, add some blue cheese crumbled on top. If you prefer it more mild, then a little goats' cheese would be delicious too.

Chocolate Banana Loaf Cake

You may be wondering – 'why on earth would you want to freeze a cake?' Well, if you're anything like me, one day the need to bake will take hold, and you'll spend all day in the kitchen, up to your elbows in eggs and flour... then, you have a surplus of cake, which, whilst delicious, means you put on a pound in a day, and then have nothing left for when you have a guest over or something... Well, now, take the initiative to freeze some of your bakes. That way, you won't over-indulge, and then, when someone pops in unexpectedly, you'll have a perfect home-made cake to offer them! (You don't have to tell them that it was homemade 6 weeks beforehand...)

Serves: 8

Preparation time: **80 minutes**

Ingredients:

For the cake:

     6 ¼ oz. sugar
- 6 ½ oz. plain flour
- 6 ½ oz. ripe bananas
- 4 tablespoons cocoa powder

- 3 ½ oz. dark chocolate chips
- 3 ¼ fl oz. vegetable oil
- 3 eggs
- 1 ½ fl oz. milk
- ½ teaspoon bicarbonate of soda
- For the frosting:
- 3 ½ oz. milk chocolate
- 3 fl oz. sour cream or yoghurt
- Dried banana chips to top

Serving suggestion:

If you don't want to put on the topping, then this is great with a scraping of coconut oil on the slice and eaten like bread.

1) Preheat the oven to 285F, and grease a loaf tin, or line it with parchment paper.

2) Mix together the flour, sugar, bicarbonate of soda, cocoa powder and chocolate chips in a bowl.

3) Mash the bananas.

4) Separate 2 of the eggs and stir in the 2 separated yolks, as well as the one remaining whole egg. Also stir in the oil and milk.

5) Stir the banana mixture into the flour mix.

6) Beat the 2 remaining egg whites, and stir a quarter of them into the mixture, before gently folding in the rest.

7) Pour the batter evenly into the loaf tin and bake for 60-70 minutes, until a skewer can be inserted and come out clean.

8) For the frosting, melt together the milk chocolate and yoghurt or sour cream and stir until smooth. Pour it over the top of the cake one it's cooled, and sprinkle on the banana chips.

9) For freezing: Allow the cake to completely cool first. Then, cling wrap it and wrap in foil. Freeze. When you want to serve

the cake, for best results, thaw in the refrigerator overnight and then allow the cake to come to room temperature.

Tips: Banana bread is so easy to make vegan, it's awesome. Due to the bananas, the eggs are not actually hugely necessary, and milk can easily be replaced by a plant-based alternative.

Ripe bananas for the win once again! Remember – the riper the banana, the sweeter and easier to mash into a smooth texture it will be!

Chicken Tikka Masala

Some days, only a curry will do! Picture the scene; it's Friday evening, you've had a long, hard week of work, and now you're looking forward to spending the evening with your feet up, enjoying a tasty dinner, sipping on a glass or 3 of wine, and catching up on the week's TV. There is no way you want to cook, but did you really work so hard all week just to throw your money at a takeout? Probably not! So, what can we do? Well, on a day when you do have the time and energy to cook, whip up this delicious chicken tikka masala. Freeze it and have it to hand for those days when you need comfort food with none of the effort!

Serves: 10

Preparation time: **50 minutes**

Ingredients:

For the masala paste:

- 5 garlic cloves
- 4 inches fresh ginger
- 4 cardamom pods
- 2 teaspoons cumin
- 2 teaspoons coriander

- 1 red chilli
- 1 teaspoon garam masala
- 1 teaspoon turmeric
- 1 teaspoon paprika

For the curry:

    28 oz. canned tomatoes
- 8 boneless, skinless chicken breasts
- 5 fl oz. yoghurt
- 5 fl oz. cream
- 4 onions
- 4 tablespoons vegetable oil
- 4 tablespoons tomato puree
- 2 red bell peppers
- 2 tablespoons mango chutney
- ¾ oz. butter
- Pinch of salt
- Chopped, fresh cilantro to serve

Serving suggestion:

Rice, of course, but also, please don't deprive yourself of fantastic naan bread to mop up the sauce!

1) First, prepare the curry paste. Chop and de-seed the chilli and peel the garlic cloves and ginger. Scrape the seeds from the cardamom pods. Then. Process together the chilli, garlic, ginger, cardamom seeds, cumin, coriander, garam masala, turmeric and paprika, adding a little water if necessary, to bring everything together into a paste.

2) Add the vegetable oil and butter into a pan to begin heating. Then, peel and dice the onion and add it into the pan to start softening, along with a pinch of salt.

3) When the onions are nice and soft, dice up the chicken and add it into the pan.

4) Chop and de-seed the bell peppers and stir them into the pan, along with 6 tablespoons of the curry paste.

5) Add in the canned tomatoes, tomato puree and ½ a cup of water, and cover the pan, leaving it to simmer for 15 minutes, until your chicken is fully cooked.

6) Remove the lid and lower the heat. Stir in the mango chutney, yoghurt and cream until everything is combined, and season with salt to taste.

7) To freeze: Place the curry immediately into the refrigerator to cool, and then place it into a freezer safe container. Ensure that all of the chicken pieces are covered in the sauce. Before enjoying, defrost by storing the curry overnight in the fridge. Then, you can microwave it or heat it in a pan.

Tips: Make a delicious vegetarian meal by using potatoes in place of the chicken.

Even if you won't make a bigger batch of curry, you can do so with the curry paste, which will freeze well, and so make a quicker and easier curry the next time.

Cheesy Vegetable Bakes

Know how to get everyone to happily eat their vegetables? Hide them underneath a mountain of delicious cheesy mashed potato! You can make this into a large, family-sized pie, or into individual bakes, perfect for popping out of the freezer as a 'ready meal' for that night in on your own that you cannot wait for!

Serves: 8

Preparation time: **90 minutes**

Ingredients:

- 53 oz. potatoes
- 28 ¾ fl oz. milk
- 17 ½ oz. leeks
- 10 ½ oz. broccoli
- 10 ½ oz. cheddar
- 6 ¼ oz. plain yoghurt
- 3 oz. butter
- 2 ½ oz. flour
- 2 teaspoons English mustard
- 1 cup frozen peas
- 1 teaspoon mustard powder

- Pinch of salt
- Pinch of pepper

Serving suggestion:

Keep this nutrient-rich by piling more veggies onto the side of this dish. If you want to treat yourself a little, why not serve with garlic bread?

1) Lightly salt a large saucepan of water and bring it to the boil.

2) Chop the broccoli into florets and slice up the leeks. Steam them above the pan of boiling water, along with the peas, until just beginning to soften.

3) Then, peel the potatoes and chop them into halves, or smaller. Add them into the saucepan for 20 minutes or so, to become tender.

4) Drain the water and mash the potatoes with salt and pepper to season. Stir in about 1/3 of the butter, along with all of the yoghurt, to create nice, smooth mash.

5) Into a new pan, add the milk, flour, English mustard, mustard powder and the rest of the butter. Whisk until smooth.

6) Grate the cheddar and stir half of it into the mixture. Then, remove the pan from the heat.

7) Divide the vegetable mix between your individual dishes, if using, or pour it all into your large, oven-proof dish.

8) Pour the sauce over the top of the dish or dishes, and the evenly spread on the mash too.

9) Sprinkle the remaining cheddar all over the top.

10) To freeze: Cover the dishes and freeze for up to 3 months. When ready to cook, preheat the oven to 360F and cook for 50-

60 minutes, until the cheese is nice and bubbly and it's warmed all the way through.

Tips: If you prefer other veggies, go ahead! A nice variation for Fall time would be using pumpkin, squash and sweet potato.

Do not over steam the vegetables, as obviously they will continue to soften as you bake the pie.

Pancakes

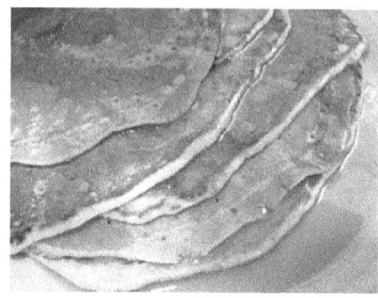

Pancakes have to be up there with the all time favourite breakfast foods of the world. If you disagree – you're wrong! The problem for me personally is that I just wish I had more mornings with enough time to spend making the little delights! Maybe pancakes wouldn't immediately pop into your head as a food that can be frozen – but, again, you would be wrong! So, when you do have the time, probably of a lazy Sunday morning, make a big old batch of pancakes and then enjoy them on Monday, and Tuesday, and all week if you like!

Makes: **20**

Preparation time: **25 minutes**

Ingredients:

- 3 cups buttermilk
- 2 eggs
- 2 tablespoons honey
- 2 tablespoons butter
- 2 teaspoons baking powder
- 1 cup plain flour
- 1 cup wholemeal flour
- 1 teaspoon baking soda

- Pinch of salt

Serving suggestion:

What pancake toppings you like is a very personal choice, I know, so I can't tell you what to do. A simple knob of butter and splash of maple syrup is always a winner. Or, cover with fresh fruit to fool, yourself into believing that you're being healthy!

1) Mix together the plain flour, wholemeal flour, baking powder, baking soda and a pinch of salt.

2) Whisk the egg, and then stir it together with the buttermilk. Then, stir the mixture into the flour mix until everything is incorporated and smooth.

3) Melt the butter and stir it into the mix, along with the honey.

4) Preheat a griddle pan, and oil it very lightly. Scoop in about ¼ of a cup of the batter at a time.

5) When you see the bubbles rising and popping, the bottom of the pancake should be done and you can scrape it up with your spatula and flip it onto the other side to fully cook through.

6) To freeze: Allow the pancakes to completely cool. Then, place them in layer on a baking tray, with parchment paper in between each layer so that they don't freeze stuck together. To re-heat, simply pop in the microwave, toaster or into a griddle until heated through!

Tips: To save space in your freezer, after a few hours when the pancakes are frozen solid, you can place them into a Ziploc bag and store them that way. They won't stick together once already frozen solid.

Buttermilk may or may not be so readily available where you are. If you want to make your own, you can simply add a tablespoon of lemon juice into regular milk and leave it to stand for 10-15 minutes.

Sweet Potato Breakfast Burritos

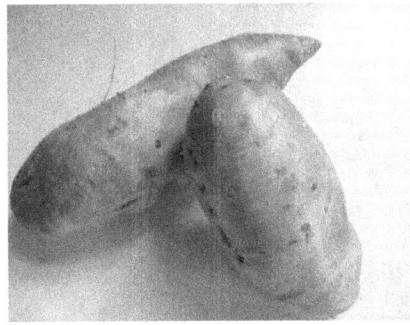

I just CANNOT get enough of sweet potatoes. I love a baked sweet potato for lunch, sweet potato fries with my dinner, even sweet potato cheesecake for dessert. So, it really is about time that the sweet potato moved its way into the breakfast zone too. So, may we introduce – the sweet potato breakfast burrito. Why a breakfast burrito? Well, we all know that breakfast is the most important meal of the day, but honestly – who has the time?? Well, heating something up as you rush around that you can then easily hold in your hand and take with you has to be a winner all round, right? So, give it a go! Oh, and did we mention, veggies for breakfast too? THAT'S how to start the day off right.

Makes: **8**

Preparation time: **50 minutes**

Ingredients:
For the hash:

- 2 garlic cloves
- 1 medium sweet potato
- 1 red bell pepper

- 1 small onion
- 1 tablespoon olive oil
- ¼ teaspoon chilli powder
- ¼ teaspoon cumin
- Pinch of salt
- Pinch of pepper

For the scrambled egg:

   8 eggs
- 2 cups spinach
- 1 tablespoon olive oil
- Pinch of salt
- Pinch of pepper

For the burrito:

   8 large tortillas
- Additional toppings of your choice egg, sour cream, fresh tomato, guacamole etc

Serving suggestion:

For me, a good burrito is a LOADED burrito! So, I would go all out with the toppings. Pack in there sour cream, guacamole, tomato salsa, shredded cheese and anything else you can think of really!

1) Let's begin by making the hash. Dice the onion and add it into a pan along with the oil to begin to soften. Then, dice the sweet potato up into ¼ inch cubes. Mince in the garlic and dice up the red bell pepper and add it into the pan too. Season well with the chilli, cumin, salt and pepper. Stir everything well so that it's mixed and reduce the heat to low for 20 minutes or so, to allow the sweet potato to become tender. Once they're done, remove the pan from the heat.

2) Next, let's scramble the eggs. Whisk the eggs and stir in the spinach and a good pinch of salt and pepper. Add a little oil into a clean pan, and then pour the mixture in. After 20 seconds or so, when the eggs begin to cook along the bottom, begin 'scrambling' them. Use a spatula to keep mixing the mixture around so that it all gets cooked but is in clumps and not a smooth omelette style. Once you're sure that the eggs are cooked through, remove the pan from the heat.

3) Now, let's assemble the burritos! Lay the tortillas our flat and add about 2 tablespoons of each of the mixture into each one. Keep the filling in a line along one side, leaving at least a 2 inch border too. Then, fold the two sides in, and fold the bottom up (this is the side with the small border next to the filling of the burrito). Wrap the bottom tightly up and over the filling and then tightly roll the tortilla all the way up.

4) To freeze: Allow the burritos to cool down to room temperature and then wrap them individually in foil and then place them into a freezer safe bag. When you want to eat your frozen burrito, simply microwave it for 60 seconds or so to warm through and you're good to go!

Tips: Rolling the burritos up can be a little tricky. A tip would be the heat the tortillas first. This makes them more pliable and less likely to break.

Now you have this down, you can customise the fillings however you like them! Try scrambled eggs with bacon and tomato salsa, or maybe chickpeas and feta cheese... the sky is the limit really!

Garlic & Lime Chicken Kebabs

Picture the scene; it's Friday evening, you've come home from work and you are feeling good! The sun is still shining and you know you're in for a beautiful long, warm evening. There is only one thing you want to do tonight – BARBECUE! What an idea! However, heading back out to the store, to come home again and prepare all of the food is time consuming and exhausting It's a good job, then, that you have some barbecue-ready chicken kebabs in your freezer just waiting to be enjoyed by you and your friends. You're so clever... give yourself a pat on the back!

Makes: 8 kebabs

Preparation time: 20 minutes + overnight marination

Ingredients:

- 8 chicken breasts
- 4 garlic cloves
- 2 limes
- ½ cup olive oil
- Pinch of salt
- Pinch of pepper

Serving suggestion:

These are so light and fresh and so go perfectly with a simple rice salad, corn on the cob, and a mojito or an ice cold beer.

1) If your chicken is not already skinless and boneless, then go ahead and de-skin and de-bone it! Then, dice it up into 1 ½ inch cubes. Place it into a Ziploc bag.

2) Juice the limes and mix the juice in with the olive oil. Mince the garlic into in too, and season well with salt and pepper.

3) Pour the lime juice mixture into the Ziploc bag with the chicken, and seal tightly, ensuring that you've squeezed all of the air out.

4) Leave the bag of chicken marinating overnight in the refrigerator.

5) The next day, thread your chicken pieces evenly onto 8 skewers.

6) To freeze: Place the skewers with the chicken still raw into a freezer safe bag. When ready to use, thaw overnight or defrost in the microwave and them grill 'em up!

Tips: This dish is 'family friendly', but, if there are no kids around, or they can really handle the heat, then what goes better with lime and garlic than chilli! Chop some red chillies up and add them into the marinade too for some extra pizzazz!

This recipe can be adapted to use pork or turkey too.

Potato Gnocchi

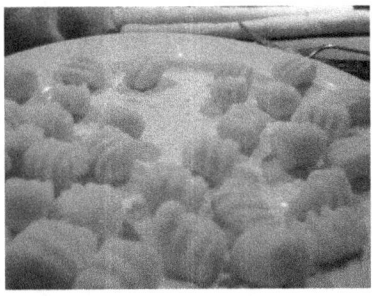

This may be another food that just does not strike you as something freezable. Hey, that's okay - that was me too! But, since I discovered that this delicious dish was freezer friendly, my cold evening dinners have been changed forever! It does have to be said that it does take a few tries to perfect gnocchi, but it will definitely be worth it! It's great to find good gnocchi in a restaurant but finding it cheap can really be a tough ask... so, being able to make good gnocchi for at home prices surely has to be the solution here?!

Serves: 4

Preparation time: **110 minutes**

Ingredients:

- 4 oz. plain flour
- 3 large russet potatoes
- 1 egg
- Pinch of salt

Serving suggestion:

This recipe will make you very good, but plain gnocchi. You can dress this up with whatever sauce or accompaniments you like!

A little burnt butter and sage sauce is always a winner, or, of course, the ever simple chunky tomato sauce, or a creamy and cheesy sauce with bacon! Whatever you like, I'm certain it'll be delicious with these little babies!

1) Preheat the oven to 400F.

2) Use a fork to spike the potatoes all over. Place the potatoes directly onto the rack in the oven and bake for 45-50 minutes, until you can easily poke a skewer all the way through them.

3) Peel the potatoes and then pass them through a potato ricer onto baking tray lined with paper towels and allow the potato to cool.

4) Weigh 16 oz. of the potato, and if you have any extra, you can save it for another use.

5) Lightly beat the egg and stir in a pinch of salt. Pour the mixture over the potato and bring together with a fork until everything is just combined.

6) Sift the flour onto the potato mix and use the fork to gently combine everything again. You don't want everything mashed together, but just be sure that no big clumps of flour are remaining.

7) Use your hands to press the dough together. Then, turn it out onto a lightly floured surface. Knead for just about a minute, turning the dough over onto itself until you have a smooth ball.

8) Divide the dough into 8 equally sized pieces, and roll each piece out into a long sausage, about ½ an inch thick.

9) Then, cut the dough up into pieces of just less than an inch in length.

10) To freeze: Place the gnocchi all spread out onto a baking tray and cover it with cling wrap. Freeze for a few hours, until the gnocchi is hardened, and then you can transfer it into a freezer safe bag to take up less room. When ready to eat, set a pan of water on to boil. Once it's boiling, drop in the gnocchi and let it cook for 2-3 minutes, until the float to the surface.

Tips: To quickly and easily peel the potatoes after baking, use a sharp knife to cut along the skin lengthways, and then just peel the skin off like a jacket!

For crispy gnocchi, after cooking, you can place it into a skillet with a little butter and get that lovely brownness around the outside.

Chicken Pot Stickers

If you haven't heard of 'pot stickers', then you may well have heard of Chinese dumplings. If you've not heard of either, then you'll have to trust me on this one that this is going to be a very, very good thing! A 'Chinese food' favourite that can be made easily at home, why not make a HUGE batch and have delicious dumplings for a snack or lunch whenever you feel like it?!

Makes: 50 dumplings

Preparation time: **30 minutes**

Ingredients:

    50 wonton wrappers
- 16 oz. ground chicken
- 3 garlic cloves
- 3 green onions
- 3 teaspoons sesame oil
- 2 tablespoons hoisin sauce
- 1 ½ teaspoons ginger paste
- 1 tablespoons vegetable oil
- Pinch of salt
- Pinch of white pepper

Serving suggestion:

These dumplings were made for dippin'! Try your hand at some classic Chinese dipping sauces to go alongside these. Why not give plum sauce a go? Or sweet and sour?

1) Place the ground chicken into a bowl. Mince the garlic and chop up the green onion. Add it into the bowl, along with the ginger paste, hoisin sauce, sesame oil and a pinch of salt and white pepper. Using your fingers is the easiest way to combine everything together.

2) Place a teaspoonful of the chicken mixture into the centre of each wonton wrapper.

3) Fill a small bowl with water, and lightly dip your finger into it. Run the wet finger along the edge of the wonton wrapper and fold it over itself to make a crescent, or triangle, depending on if you use round or square wrappers. Pinch the edges together, ensuring that there is no trapped air.

4) Heat the oil in a large pan and add in the pot stickers in a single layer. Leave them cooking until golden, for about 2 minutes

5) To freeze: Place the pot stickers onto a baking tray lined with parchment paper and freeze for a couple of hours until solid. Then, you can transfer them into a freezer safe bag and microwave to re-heat when you're ready to eat them! You can also freeze them uncooked, and then give them an extra 2 minutes cooking time when you're heating them. Use the pan!

Tips: Make a vegetarian version by replacing the ground chicken with shredded cabbage or carrot.

You can also boil pot stickers to cook them through, but why you wouldn't want them crispy is a mystery to me!

Lentil Chilli

Looking for a hearty, flavoursome meal that all the family will LOVE? Do you have the constant struggle with the purse strings, though? Are you desperate to get your family eating 'healthy'? I'm fairly certain that the answer to all three of the above questions was yes? Yes again? And again?! Okay, I'll stop now, but I have to let you know that this lentil chilli is the answer to everything!

Serves: 8

Preparation time: **50 minutes**

Ingredients:

- 32 oz. vegetable stock
- 16 oz. brown lentils
- 14 oz. canned diced tomatoes
- 5 garlic cloves
- 4 teaspoons chilli powder
- 2 tablespoons oil
- 1 onion
- 1 red bell pepper
- 1 bay leaf
- Pinch of salt

- Pinch of pepper

Serving suggestion:

I feel like there are 2 ways of eating chilli. You can go down the more 'Latino' route of serving it with rice, or, you can go full on cowboy and serve it just as it is, but topped with sour cream, bacon bits, shredded cheese, green onions and Jalapeños. Both are good, so the choice is yours.

1) Begin heating the olive oil in a large pot.

2) Peel and dice the onion, and de-seed and dice the red bell pepper. Add them into the pan with the oil to begin to soften.

3) After 5 minutes or so, mince in the garlic and stir it in along with the chilli powder.

4) Then, after another 2-3 minutes, pour in the lentils, tomatoes and vegetable stock, and add the bay leaf too.

5) Leave it simmering, covered for about 30 minutes, until the lentils are tender. Remove the bay leaf.

6) Remove 3 cups out of the chilli and blend it in a food processor. Stir it back in and season with salt and pepper to taste.

7) To freeze: Allow the chilli to cool and then transfer it to a freezer safe container. When you're ready to re-heat, just pop it in the microwave until it's warmed through and there you have it!

Tips: Do check that the lentils are tender and leave them to keep on cooking if necessary. Having undercooked lentils is never, I repeat NEVER a good thing!

Chop up and add in as many more veggies as you like too! Carrot works well or blending up zucchini and eggplant to stir into the chilli is a great way to sneak in that goodness!

Winter Vegetable Soup

Having something 'frozen' for dinner may be that last thing that sounds appealing when, during the winter, you've spent all day doing just that yourself – freezing! If you're anything like me though, when you blow in through the door and bolt it behind you on a cold, dark and stormy winter's night, you do not want to be cooking. You want to get something warm inside you and snuggle up on the couch with a feel-good movie and your favourite slippers! So, having soup that simply needs reheating and is ready to go is a very, very good idea indeed!

Serves: 8

Preparation time: **40 minutes**

Ingredients:

    6 green onions
- 4 leeks
- 4 celery stalks
- 4 medium potatoes

- 3 parsnips
- 3 sweet potatoes
- 2 cups vegetable stock
- 2 tablespoons oil
- 1 sprig dried thyme
- 1 cup coconut milk
- Pinch of salt
- Pinch of pepper

Serving suggestion:

There is only one thing you need with an awesome soup like this – fresh bread!

1) Begin heating the oil in a large saucepan.

2) Rinse the leeks and celery and shop them into 'half moons' (slice them in half lengthways and then chop up). Also, peel and dice the parsnips and chop up the green onion. Toss it all into the pan to begin tenderising for 8 minutes.

3) Meanwhile, chop up the sweet potatoes and potatoes. You can peel them too if you like, but as long as you scrub the skin well, you can save yourself a job.

4) Add into the pot the potatoes, sweet potatoes, vegetable stock and thyme, and season well with salt and pepper.

5) Bring the pan to the boil, and then reduce it down to a simmer and cover the pot.

6) Leave it simmering for 10-12 minutes whilst the potatoes cook through.

7) Then, stir in the coconut milk and leave it heating through for just another couple of minutes. Season again with salt and pepper to taste, if necessary, and remove the thyme.

8) To freeze: Simply allow the soup to cool to room temperature and transfer it into a freezer safe container or baggies. When you want to eat it, simply heat in the microwave or in a pan.

Tips: You could ladle the soup into individual baggies for a one person portion whenever you need it – you could even take it to work for a healthy winter-time lunch.

The vegetables you can use are not limited to only this selection! The ones we chose are, as the name suggests, great 'winter vegetables', but of course you can add in whatever you like!

'Monkey Tails'

Healthy eating, a lot of the time is not to challenging. The time that I always struggle with, though, is mid-afternoon. I'm talking those three o clock blues. Work is dragging, I need a coffee and I am just CRAVING some sugar! This is very often when all of my good work throughout the day goes to pot, and I end up with a chocolate bar or a cheeky cake from the bakery... well, here is a great way to get your sugar rush but keep it healthy too – monkey tails! So, named, not because, as you may have guessed, they are actually literal monkey tails, but because they just happen to resemble them, in a way – and it's much more fun to say than 'bananas dipped in chocolate'.

Makes: **12**

Preparation time: 10 minutes + at least 2 hours freezing

Ingredients:

    6 bananas
- 2 cups dark chocolate chips
- 2 cups toppings – e.g. granola, poppy seeds, pistachios, peanuts, dried cranberries etc

Serving suggestion:

It's mid-afternoon, so a coffee probably wouldn't go amiss either...

1) Chop your bananas in half, and stick a popsicle stick into it, from the cut end upwards.

2) Place the bananas into a freezer safe container and allow them to freeze solid for about 2 hours, until hard.

3) Melt the chocolate chips and set out your toppings of choice.

4) Roll each banana popsicle in the melted chocolate and then roll it in or sprinkle on your toppings.

5) To freeze: Place the bananas back into a freezer safe container and allow to freeze solid. Then, enjoy frozen on a hot day, or remove them and place them in the refrigerator to thaw.

Tips: Working quickly is advised, simply because the frozen banana will cause the chocolate to harden pretty quickly, which may lead to topping problems...

Try to work with bananas that are just ripe. You want the sweetness, but being too ripe leads to squishiness and will just make them harder to skewer and keep in shape etc. Go for the day after they turn yellow would be my advice!

Raspberry Cheesecake Squares

Everyone is a fan of cheesecake, come on! I am also a fan of ice cream... and sometimes I know that I really shouldn't just eat both... So, what about a cheesecake that gets frozen so kind of becomes ice cream in its own special way? I call that 'killing two birds with one stone'! Making a rectangular cheesecake and then chopping it up into individual squares makes storage in the freezer much easier, and then – you have cheesecake ready and waiting for you in the freezer! It must be done!

Makes: **16**

Preparation time: **5 minutes**

Ingredients:
For the crust:

    10 oz. cookies or Graham crackers
- 1 teaspoon vanilla extract
- ½ cup pecans
- ½ cup butter

For the filling:

24 oz. cream cheese
- 4 eggs
- 1 ½ cups sugar
- 1 ½ teaspoons vanilla extract
- ½ cup sour cream

For the topping:

4 cups raspberries
- 2 tablespoons corn starch
- 1 cup sugar

Serving suggestion:

If it's the evening, then why not a little raspberry-flavoured tipple to go alongside... I'm thinking a raspberry mojito... or a glass of bubbly with raspberries popped into it... or whatever else you can come up with!

1) Preheat the oven to 350F and line a baking tray with parchment paper.

2) Pulse together the cookies and pecans into a fine crumb.

3) Melt the butter and drizzle it in to the crumb mixture, along with the vanilla extract, until it comes together.

4) Press the crumb mixture firmly and evenly down into the pan.

5) Beat together the cream cheese and the vanilla extract for the filling.

6) Beat the eggs in one at a time, and then fold in the sour cream until everything is nice and smooth.

7) Pour the cream cheese filling on top of the crust and spread it out evenly.

8) Bake it in the oven for 45 minutes. Then, turn the oven off and leave the cheesecake in there for another 10 minutes. Open the oven door and leave it sitting there for a final 10 minutes.

9) Into a saucepan, add the raspberries, sugar and ¼ of a cup of sugar. 'Smash' the raspberries slightly to being releasing some of the juices.

10) Bring it to the boil so that the juices can thicken for about 5 minutes.

11) Stir the cornstarch and about 4 tablespoons of water together, and then stir it into the raspberry mixture.

12) Bring the mixture to the boil for another 2 minutes or so, and then remove it from the heat.

13) Pour the raspberry mix over the baked cheesecake and place it into the freezer to set for about an hour.

14) To freeze: Once it's set, you can go in and cut it up into individual squares, before placing them into a freezer safe container. To eat, either enjoy frozen or place in the refrigerator to thaw before enjoying.

Tips: If raspberries aren't your favourite, you can try with any other kind of berries, such as strawberries, blueberries or blackberries.

For the smoothest cheesecake mix in the land, use room temperate cream cheese.

Mint Brownies

So, 'frozen' brownies, I agree is a weird concept, but get this – they don't actually freeze solid. Instead, they become somehow even MORE fudge-y and delicious than they already were, and instead of a winter warmer, they can become a fantastic cool summer snack!

Makes: **18+**

Preparation time: **60 minutes**

Ingredients:

- 10 eggs
- 8 oz. cream cheese
- 3 1/3 cups sugar
- 2 cups butter
- 2 cups plain flour
- 2 teaspoons vanilla extract
- 1 ½ cups cocoa powder
- 1 ½ tablespoons peppermint extract
- 1 cup dark chocolate chips
- 1 teaspoon baking powder
- Pinch of salt
- A few drops of green food colouring

Serving suggestion:

PERFECT chopped up into little pieces and swirled into your ice cream! (love-heart eye emoji!)

1) Preheat the oven to 350F and line a large baking tray with parchment paper.

2) Melt the butter in a pan, stirring constantly so that it doesn't stick. Then, remove it from the heat and stir in the chocolate chips and 3 cups of sugar until smooth.

3) Then, add in 8 of the eggs, one at a time, stirring each one in completely before adding the next. Also, stir in the vanilla extract.

4) Stir in the flour, cocoa powder, baking powder and a pinch of salt, just until everything is incorporated. Set the batter aside.

5) Beat together the cream cheese, 2 remaining eggs, mint extract and a few drops of green food colouring until the mixture is smooth and is your desired colour.

6) Pour about 2/3 of the brownie batter into the baking tray. Then, roughly spread the mint cream cheese mixture over the top, before pouring on the remaining brownie batter.

7) Bake for 25-45 minutes (depending on your oven! I don't want to give you a time that will lead to over-baked brownies, because that would be super sad! Just keep checking on them!)

8) To freeze: Allow the brownies to cool completely before cutting them up into individual squares. Wrap each brownie in cling wrap and freeze. Then, simply enjoy straight from the freezer!

Tips: To make these brownies aesthetically as well as 'to your taste buds' pleasing, before baking, use a knife to swirl the cream cheese and brownie batter together a little to create a nice marbling effect.

Of course, you can use a shop bought brownie mix, but just know that I will be judging you! This recipe is just tried and tested fudge-y perfection, so we know it will be good!

Cottage Pie

Ahh, cottage pie... If you're from, shall we say, 'cooler climes', then this, I'm sure will be up there with those meals that you just NEED to eat when you get in from the cold. It's also, in my opinion, a perfect candidate for 'batch cooking' – making an extra 1 or 2 (or more!) to freeze for a quick but tasty and nourishing meal on those days when you just can't! Meat and vegetable casserole or stew is topped with delicious mashed potato and cheese... yeah, it doesn't get much better than this...

Serves: 8

Preparation time: **85 minutes**

Ingredients:

- 48 oz. potatoes
- 24 oz. ground beef
- 16 oz. onions
- 4 tablespoons butter
- 2 cups chicken broth
- 2 tablespoons olive oil
- 1 butternut squash
- 1 cup frozen peas

- 1 cup milk
- 1 cup shredded cheese
- 1 tablespoon Worcestershire sauce
- ¼ cup plain flour
- ¼ cup tomato paste
- Pinch of salt
- Pinch of pepper

Serving suggestion:

Extra steamed veggies (broccoli, carrots, green beans...) and a swimming pool of beef gravy is the way to do this.

1) Preheat the oven to 350F.

2) Peel the potatoes and then place them into a large saucepan and cover them with water to an inch above them. Bring the pan to the boil and add a pinch of salt. Then, reduce it down to a simmer and leave them to become tender.

3) Strain the potatoes and return them to the pot, and add in the milk and butter, as well as a good dash of salt and pepper. Mash them, getting down to as few lumps as possible! You can add a little extra milk or butter if need be.

4) Add a little oil into a pan. Peel and dice the onion and add it into the pan to begin browning. After 5 minutes or so, transfer them to a bowl.

5) Into the same pan, add a little more oil if necessary, and then add in the ground beef. Season with salt and pepper and use a spoon to be breaking it up as it browns for 5 minutes.

6) Then, mix in the tomato paste, Worcestershire sauce and the flour and stir everything well.

7) Peel and dice the squash.

8) Then, add in the broth, squash, the cooked onions and the frozen peas and bring the mixture to the simmer.

9) Once the mixture has reduced down, pour it into a deep oven proof casserole dish.

10) Dollop the mashed potato all over the top of the beef, smoothing it and spreading it with a spatula to ensure an even covering.

11) Place the dish into the oven to bake for 40-45 minutes so that the mash is nicely crisped up on top. 5-10 minutes before removing from the oven, sprinkle on the cheese and allow it to melt before serving.

12) To freeze: You can bake it completely and then allow to cool and then freeze it. Simply bake from frozen. Or, if you prefer, you can freeze before baking and then just start from there. The choice is yours!

Tips: I love adding a little something extra to the mash, personally. Why not stir in a little mustard for a kick to your potato?

Also, the sky is the limit when it comes to vegetables, am I right? So just go ahead and add whatever else you like into the beef mixture and get in all of those vitamins!

Shrimp Stir Fry

The time has come for a slightly different type of 'freezer meal'. Instead of cooking ahead and freezing for re-heating, we are simply going to prepare everything, freeze it, and then cook it fresh when you're ready to serve. Don't worry though, the cooking will still only take a matter of minutes! What's great about not cooking this dish first actually, is that during freezing, the shrimp keeps on marinating and so your flavour will just keep on getting better!

Serves: 4

Preparation time: **15 minutes**

Ingredients:

24 oz. shrimp
- 3 garlic cloves
- 3 cups broccoli florets
- 3 tablespoons soy sauce
- 2 carrots
- 2 tablespoons oyster sauce
- 1 bell pepper
- 1 green onion (to serve)
- 1 cup sugar snap peas

- 1 tablespoon olive oil (to serve)
- 1 tablespoon white wine vinegar
- 1 tablespoon brown sugar
- 1 tablespoon fresh ginger
- 1 teaspoon sesame seeds (to serve)
- 1 teaspoon sesame oil
- 1 teaspoon sriracha
- 1 teaspoon cornstarch

Serving suggestion:

Noodles or rice are both super simple and easy to whip up with this dish.

1) In a bowl, mix together the sesame oil, soy sauce, oyster sauce, brown sugar, white wine vinegar, fresh ginger, cornstarch and Sriracha. Mince in the garlic too and stir everything well.

2) Check that your shrimp are all peeled and de-veined. If they're not, doing it now will make the meal much more enjoyable! Then, add the shrimps into the sauce and toss them around a bit to get them coated.

3) De-seed and chop up the bell pepper, and peel and julienne the carrots.

4) Into a large Ziploc bag, pour the shrimp mixture, along with all of the sauce, and then add in the bell pepper, carrots, sugar snap peas and broccoli.

5) To freeze: Squeeze the air out of your Ziploc bag and seal it tightly. Freeze until you are ready to enjoy it! Then, simply place a little olive oil in a pan and dump the whole bag in. Stir occasionally, until you are sure that the shrimp is cooked through (7-10 minutes) and garnish with chopped green onion and sesame seeds.

Tips: If you're going to be using noodles, you can even freeze them in the bag too.

Do we really careful with shrimp. It can be bad if undercooked, so really do check it through before serving.

Cheese & Ham Stuffed Chicken

Cheese & ham really is just one of the all-time great flavour combinations. I know that other things may be more sophisticated, or seem a little more classy, but there are some days when you want your food to be giving you a hug from the inside, and that is what cheese and ham will do for you! This dish is the perfect candidate for the old 'cook for dinner and freeze the leftovers' trick. Just make sure you have enough self control to actually leave some leftovers!

Serves: 12

Preparation time: **60 minutes**

Ingredients:

    12 boneless chicken breasts
- 11 fl oz. cream of chicken soup
- 6 slices ham
- 6 slices Swiss cheese
- ½ cup chicken broth
- ½ teaspoon sage
- ¼ cup plain flour
- ¼ cup grated parmesan
- ¼ cup vegetable oil

- ¼ teaspoon paprika
- Pinch of salt
- Pinch of pepper

Serving suggestion:

Well, it's probably going to be potatoes and veg, but which variation of each you choose is entirely up to you! Keep is light and summery with new potatoes and salad or go for a winter warmer with mash and steamed broccoli and carrots.

1) If not already done, slice the chicken breasts into halves. Then, using a meat cleaver, smash them down to less than ½ an inch thickness.

2) Onto each half of chicken breast, layer a slice of ham and then a slice of Swiss cheese.

3) Begin at one end and tightly roll the chicken breast over itself to create a roll. Use a toothpick to secure it and keep it together.

4) In a separate bowl, combine the flour, parmesan, paprika, sage and a pinch of salt and pepper. Coat the chicken in this mixture.

5) Place the chicken in a skillet for a few minutes to begin browning, turn it over to get an even cooking. Then, transfer it into an oven safe casserole dish.

6) Combine the chicken soup and chicken broth, and season to taste, if necessary. Pour the mixture all over the chicken.

7) Bake at 350F for 25-35 minutes. Check obviously, that the chicken is cooked through before serving.

8) To freeze: Let the chicken come to room temperature and then transfer it into a freezer safe container. When you want to use it, place it in the refrigerator overnight to thaw, and then

just reheat all the way through in a skillet. Obviously, check that it definitely is re-heated all the way through again before serving!

Tips: You can use other types of cheese, of course, but I thought I would play it safe with the fairly mild Swiss. If you're really big on that cheesy flavour, then go for something more pungent!

If you want to make a double batch to freeze some, then you could even leave one dish unbaked. Simply store the mixture in a freezer safe container and leave it in the refrigerator to thaw overnight. Then, bake until cooked through. It will take a little longer if it's not fully thawed, so do be careful to check it thoroughly.

Pepperoni Pizza Puffs

So why would you want to have a freezer full of pepperoni pizza puffs? Well, have you ever been invited to a 'bring a plate' type gathering, and forgotten about your 'plate' until a very short time beforehand? I know I most certainly have! So, having a little supply of great finger food in the freezer would be very useful, am I right...? And, let's be honest, anything vaguely pizza related is always a crowd pleaser!

Makes: **24**

Preparation time: **40 minutes**

Ingredients:

- 2 tablespoons chopped fresh basil
- 1 egg
- 1 red bell pepper
- 1 garlic clove
- 1 cup shredded mozzarella
- 1 cup sliced pepperoni
- ¾ cup plain flour
- ¾ cup milk
- ¾ teaspoon baking powder
- ½ cup canned tomatoes

- ½ teaspoon oregano
- Pinch of salt
- Pinch of pepper

Serving suggestion:

If you just CAN'T face making dinner one evening, why not thaw a couple of these and serve with simple potato wedges and salad?

1) Preheat the oven to 375F and grease a 24 cup muffin tin.

2) Stir together the flour and baking powder, and then whisk in the egg and milk.

3) De-seed and chop up the bell pepper.

4) Stir the mozzarella, bell pepper and pepperoni through the mixture and set it aside for 10 minutes.

5) Bake the pizza puffs for 20-25 minutes until they are well-risen and golden.

6) Meanwhile, you can make your dipping sauce. Into a pan, add the canned tomatoes and stir through the oregano and basil, along with salt and pepper to taste. Blend the sauce until smooth.

7) To freeze: Allow the puffs to cool, and then place them into a freezer safe container. If there will be more than one layer, add a sheet of parchment paper in between them so that they don't stick together. Transfer the dipping sauce into a separate container. When ready to serve, simply thaw everything in the refrigerator and re-heat in the microwave, or you can bake the puffs for 5 minutes or so.

Tips: I have just made a basic tomato sauce, but I also love to do a hot and spicy version with chilli, if you know there won't be unsuspecting children!

Also, you can make this vegetarian. Simply remove the pepperoni and add in any other vegetables that you like!

Vegetarian Moussaka

Let's get middle-eastern! I first encountered moussaka in Greek and Turkish restaurants, but it is also widely enjoyed going further east, and into Asia. Moussaka, if you haven't had it before, is fairly similar to its Italian cousin, lasagne, and it a good, hearty and healthy vegetarian meal packed full of veggies. It's the perfect way to fool your family into eating those things that are good for them!

Serves: 12

Preparation time: **120 minutes**

Ingredients:

- 28 oz. canned chickpeas
- 28 oz. canned tomatoes
- 28 oz. potatoes
- 5 black peppercorns
- 4 eggplants
- 4 bay leaves
- 3 ½ oz. brown lentils
- 3 cups milk
- 2 ½ oz. butter
- 2 ½ oz. flour
- 2 onions

- 2 garlic cloves
- 2 eggs
- 1 ¾ oz. feta
- 1 ¾ oz. mozzarella
- 1 sprig fresh rosemary
- 1 sprig fresh sage
- 1 cup red wine
- 1 tablespoon olive oil
- 1 teaspoon dried oregano
- Pinch of salt
- Pinch of pepper

Serving suggestion:

This is such a great 'all in one' dish. Maybe just some fresh bread to dip into the delicious leftover sauce is all you'll need. And a glass of red wine to wash it all down.

1) Preheat the oven to 350F.

2) Peel and dice the onion, and peel and mince the garlic and add them into a large pan with the olive oil.

3) Add in the rosemary, sage and oregano. Leave the onions and garlic to fry and soften for about 7 minutes.

4) Pour in the wine and turn the heat up to high, so that the mixture is bubbling.

5) After 5 minutes or so, stir in the chickpeas, including their water, the tomatoes, the lentils and 2 of the bay leaves.

6) Season with salt and pepper to taste and bring the mixture to the boil. Then, reduce the heat to low and leave the mixture simmering for about an hour.

7) Meanwhile, you can slice up the eggplants into roughly ¼ of an inch thick slices. Sprinkle them with salt and then leave to one side, soaking in water.

8) Also slice up the potatoes to ¼ of an inch thick and add them into a pan of boiling salted water for just 5 minutes to begin becoming tender.

9) Drain the potatoes, and then spread them out in a layer in the bottom of a deep casserole dish. Season with salt and pepper, and drizzle on some olive oil, and then bake for 35 minutes.

10) Rinse the eggplants and do the same as with the potatoes – sprinkle with salt, pepper and oil, and roast them for 35 minutes.

11) In a pan separate from the lentil mixture, begin heating the milk with the 2 remaining bay leaves and the peppercorns. Stir it as it simmers, but don't let it come to the boil. Then, remove the mixture from the pan, and add in the butter to melt.

12) Stir the flour into the melted butter to form a paste, and then add in the hot milk mixture, a little at a time, stirring as you go. Remove the bay leaves and peppercorns as you go.

13) Once the mixture is smooth, add in 1/3 of the feta and 1/3 of the mozzarella and simmer and stir until you have a smooth and glossy béchamel.

14) It's time to assemble the moussaka! Onto the potatoes in their casserole dish, spoon half of the tomato mixture. Then, layer on half of the eggplants and top with the remaining tomato mix. Layer on the remaining eggplants. Separate the eggs, and whisk the yolks into your béchamel sauce, then, quickly pour it all over the top of your moussaka. Sprinkle on the remaining feta

and mozzarella, and then bake for 35 minutes until everything is golden and bubbling.

15) To freeze: Leave the moussaka to cool to room temperature and then transfer into a freezer safe container before freezing. Then, you can simply re-heat individual portions in the microwave, or bake the dish again for 5 minutes.

Tips: I know that store bought béchamel and tomato sauces are available, but I do 100% recommend making your own. You will know exactly what has gone in there, you can get it tasting exactly as you like it, and you just cannot get that same sense of satisfaction from opening a jar!

It's good to know too, that you can freeze those egg whites that you didn't use and make them into something else delicious at a later time!

Creamy Chicken Pesto Pasta

I cannot count the number of times that pesto pasta has been an absolute life-saver for me! It's a favourite of all the family, and it super quick and easy to do. You know what else is great about this pasta...? It works fantastically as a freezer meal! I even think that sometimes, it is better the second time around – reheating in a pan gives you those little crispy bits that are just to die for!

Serves: 4

Preparation time: **60 minutes**

Ingredients:

For the pesto:

   3 cups fresh basil
- 1 garlic clove
- 1/3 cup pine nuts
- ¼ cup olive oil
- Pinch of salt
- Pinch of pepper

For the pasta:

   8 oz. fettuccine or other pasta
- 3 chicken breasts

- 1 tablespoon olive oil
- ¼ cup cream
- Pinch of salt
- Pinch of pepper

Serving suggestion:

I, for one, have absolutely no problem with carbs on carbs – garlic bread all the way!

1) First, let's make the pesto; spread the pine nuts out on a baking tray and toast them at 350F for 4 minutes. Bring 2 cups of salted water to the boil, and quickly submerge the basil and remove it immediately into a colander to drain. Process together the basil, pine nuts, garlic clove, and a pinch of salt. When the nuts are chopped, add in the olive oil in a steady stream, keeping on processing until everything is smooth.

2) Set your pasta to cook according to the package instructions. When it's done, keep aside ¼ of a cup of the cooking liquid.

3) Halve the chicken breasts, and pound them down to ¼ inch thickness. Chop into strips.

4) Add the olive oil into a pan and place the chicken in, seasoning it with salt and pepper. Cook for 3-5 minutes, until golden brown.

5) Into the pan where the chicken in, add the pesto and cream, as well as the ¼ cup of pasta water. Season to taste and serve poured over the pasta.

6) To freeze: There are 2 ways of doing this – 1) make the pasta all together and then simply allow it to cool to room temperature, divide it into freezer safe bags, and reheat in the microwave or in a pan when you're ready! 2) Make ahead a big

batch of pesto and freeze it in ice cube trays. Then, you can make this dish fresh using about 4 cubes of the frozen pesto.

Tips: Pesto is DELISH! And so easy to make. You can make a tonne of variations on it too. All you really need is a nut, a green leaf, garlic and an oil – the possibilities are endless!

As with pretty much any pasta dish, sprinkling with cheese will be a delight.

Sweet Potato, Spinach & Chickpea Curry

I know it's a big thing to say, but curry could well be my favourite dish... Of course, there is a humongous scope of dishes that come under the umbrella of 'curry', and so I'm not limiting myself here! I love that a curry can really be anything you want it to be – can be full of whatever ingredients you like and can taste as mild or as spicy as you wish. Here, I have taken some of my personal favourite ingredients and turned them into a delicious and fairly mild chilli that is sure to please pretty much everyone. Best part is, of course, that you can freeze it and enjoy it again too!

Serves: 6

Preparation time: **60 minutes**

Ingredients:

For the curry paste:

     3 inches fresh ginger
- 2 garlic cloves
- 2 tablespoons peanut oil
- 2 tablespoons tomato paste
- 2 tablespoons garam masala
- 2 teaspoons cumin seeds

- 2 teaspoons coriander seeds
- 1 chilli
- 1 tablespoon paprika
- 1 tablespoon smoked paprika
- 1 tablespoon turmeric
- 1 teaspoon black peppercorns
- ¼ cup fresh cilantro
- Pinch of salt

For the curry:

14 oz. chickpeas
- 14 oz. tomatoes
- 14 oz. spinach
- 14 fl oz. coconut milk
- 3 sweet potatoes
- 2 red onions
- 2 inches fresh ginger
- 2 tablespoons olive oil
- 1 red chilli
- 1/3 cup fresh coriander

Serving suggestion:

Just good old sticky rice will do!

Let's make the curry paste first;

1) Into a dry frying pan on high heat add the coriander seeds, cumin seeds and black peppercorns to begin toasting for a few minutes until they become fragrant.

2) Add the spices into a pestle and mortar or food processor and grind them up. Peel and grate the ginger and garlic and chop up the chilli. Then, blend the ground spice mix up with the ginger, garlic, peanut oil, tomato paste, garam masala, chilli, paprika, smoked paprika, cilantro and a pinch of salt until smooth.

3) Begin heating the oil in a pan. Peel and dice the onion and add it into the pan, along with 3 tablespoons of the curry paste and allow it to cook down for 10 minutes.

4) Chop up the chilli and grate the fresh ginger. Roughly chop up the cilantro too and chop the sweet potato into 1 inch chunks.

5) Add the chilli, ginger, cilantro and sweet potato into the pan. Drain the canned chickpeas and add them in too.

6) Roughly chop up the tomatoes and tip them into the pan too. Also add in ¾ of a cup of water and bring the mixture to the boil.

7) Then, reduce it down to a simmer and leave the pot covered for 10-15 minutes. Remove the lid and cook for a further 10-15 minutes, whilst the sweet potatoes become tender.

8) Then, stir in the coconut milk and the spinach until the spinach is wilted.

9) To freeze: Allow the curry to cool and then place it in a freezer safe container. You can then just reheat in the microwave.

Tips: You'll have some curry paste leftover (yay!) This can also be frozen and sued to make another delicious curry at a later date.

This is vegetarian (obviously) but if you're looking to add something, my suggestion would be shrimp.

Part 2

Introduction

Cook up a storm when you feel like it. Freeze. And pop it in the microwave or a crockpot to enjoy a gourmet, home cooked meal without the fuss. That is the beauty of freezer meals. Below is a collection of soups, stews, casseroles, entrees, breakfast meals and snacks that you can make ahead and readily enjoy when you feel like it. It's easy, fast and very convenient.

Read through our proven tips and tricks for make-ahead, freezable recipes:

On storage:
- Don't tie up your fancy casserole dishes or baking pans—instead, use foil baking pans, plastic freezer bags, resealable bags or disposable plastic containers.
- Label your freezer meals—it will make it easier to figure out which is which when they are ready to be served.
- Allow your recipes to cool down before placing them in the freezer. It may cause your recipe to freeze unevenly and cause spoiling.
- To cook hot food quickly, place a pan in a sink filled with ice water. Make sure water doesn't get into the soup.
- Divide each batch of your freezer meals into individual, meal-sized portions—label and date them.
- Wrap your food tightly and well—use special freezer wrappers that are vapor- and moisture-proof.
- When freezing liquids, leave room for expansion before putting the lid on or wrapping.
- Remove as much air from the bag as possible when using freezer bags before sealing.
- For solid foods, wrap in foil first before bagging them and placing in the freezer.

Freezing can conveniently preserve food, but not forever, Eventually, the flavor and quality of the food will be affected. Here's a quick cheat sheet on how long certain recipes will keep in the freezer for best results:

Tomato- or vegetable-based sauces   6 months

Meat-based loaf recipes   6 months

Soups and stews   2-3 months

Casseroles 6 months

Dry poultry   6 months

Poultry with sauce   3 months

Meatballs in sauce   6 months

Pizza dough   3-4 weeks

Once your food is ready to be enjoyed, here's how you can safely thaw it:

- Pop it in the refrigerator and allow it to thaw inside. This process takes longer—generally, it takes about 24 hours—but it is one of the safest ways to defrost frozen food.
- Place the frozen food in a liquid-proof bag and place it in a container with cold water.
- Pop it in the microwave and thaw it.

Delicious Freezer Recipes

Recipes Included In This Book

Baked Chicken Nuggets

Beef and Noodle Casserole

Cheesy Veggie Chowder

Creamy Chicken Casserole

Burrito Bake

Cheesy Greens Roll Ups

Chicken, Ham and Cheese Casserole

Cheesy Ham and Potatoes

Make Ahead Mac and Cheese

Classic Pot Roast

Chicken Parmiagiana Bake

Make Ahead Mongolian Beef

Breakfast Burritos

Beef and Mushrooms

All-American Casserole

Veggie and Mozzarella Farfalle

Homemade Frozen Pizza

Easy Bake Chicken Pot Pie

Creamy Chicken and Salsa

Baked Spaghetti

Buttermilk Pancakes

Creamy Parmesan Chicken Penne

Baked Pork Chops

Turkey Loaf

Lemon Garlic Chicken

Freezer Recipes

Baked Chicken Nuggets

Prep Time: 35 minutes

Servings: **4-6**

Ingredients:

3 cups corn flakes

1/3 cup grated Parmesan cheese

1/2 teaspoon salt

1/4 teaspoon onion powder

1/4 teaspoon garlic powder

A pinch of pepper

1 pound chicken breasts, deboned

1/4 cup flour

2 large eggs, beaten

Directions:
1. Chop chicken into small, 2" pieces and set aside.

2. Crush cornflakes in a plastic bag and add salt, onion and garlic powder, pepper and Parmesan cheese.
3. Dip chicken in egg and place in the cornflake mixture. Shake bag until coated well.
4. Repeat until you have gone through all ingredients.
5. Arrange carefully in a freezer bag and place in a freezer until ready to cook.
6. To cook, thaw nuggets and bake until brown at 425 degrees in an oven.

Beef And Noodle Casserole

Prep Time: **30 minutes**

Servings: **6**

Ingredients:

1 pound of ground beef, browned

1 jar pre-made spaghetti sauce

1 (8 ounce) package cream cheese

1/4 cup sour cream

1 (8 ounce) tub cottage cheese

1 (8 ounce) pack spaghetti noodles, cooked

1 cup of cheddar cheese, shredded

Directions:
1. In a saucepan, combine sour cream, cream cheese and cottage cheese. Stir well and mix thoroughly.
2. Place spaghetti noodles in a foil tray.
3. Pour cream sauce over it and mix well.
4. Top with ground beef and spaghetti sauce.
5. Cover tightly and allow to cool before popping in the freezer.
6. To cook—thaw and bake in an oven at 350 degrees until heated through.

Cheesy Veggie Chowder

Prep Time: **30 minutes**

Servings: **4-6**

Ingredients:

2 vegetable bouillon cubes

1 cup water

1 cup diced celery

2 cups diced potatoes

1 cup diced carrot

1 (10 ounce) package mixed vegetables

1 (10-ounce) can cream of chicken soup

1 can of milk

1 pound (16 ounces) Velveeta cheese, cubed

Directions:
1. Combine water, celery, potatoes, carrots and bouillon cubes in a stock pot.
2. Stir and simmer until dissolved.
3. Add vegetables and lower heat. Allow to cook fro 30-40 minutes before adding milk, chicken soup and cheese.
4. Keep stirring until cheese has melted.
5. Allow to cool and transfer to a freezer-safe container.
6. To serve—pop in a microwave to thaw and heat over medium fire on stove.

Creamy Chicken Casserole

Prep Time: **20 minutes**

Servings: **6**

Ingredients:

2 cups chicken, cooked and diced

2 cups wheat crackers, crushed

1 tablespoon poppy seeds

1 (10 ounce) can cream of chicken soup

1 1/2 cups sour cream

1/2 cup butter, melted

1 teaspoon Worcestershire sauce

1 teaspoon minced garlic

1 tablespoon lemon juice

Directions:
1. Combine soup, chicken and sour cream in a bowl. Mix well.
2. Add garlic and lemon juice with Worcestershire sauce.
3. In a separate bowl, mix poppy seeds, crackers and butter.
4. Pour chicken mixture in a baking pan and top with cracker mixture.
5. Cover tightly and place in a freezer.
6. Once ready to cook—thaw and bake in the oven set at 350 degrees for 40 minutes.

Burrito Bake

Prep Time: **40 minutes**

Servings: **6-12**

Ingredients:

2 pounds ground beef

1 onion, diced

2 teaspoons garlic, minced

1 can black olives, sliced

1 can diced green chiles, drained

1 can diced tomatoes, drained

2 cans refried beans

12 flour tortillas

1 jar enchilada sauce

2 cups cheddar cheese, shredded

Directions:
1. Sauté ground beef until browned with onions and garlic.
2. Remove excess fat and mix in peppers, olives, tomatoes and enchilada sauce.
3. Allow mixture to simmer for 20 minutes.
4. Assemble burritos by spreading refried beans onto a wrapper, top with meat mixture and sprinkle cheese on top and wrapping it. Repeat until you have gone through all the tortillas.
5. Arrange burritos carefully, seam side down on an aluminum baking tray. Top with remaining meat sauce and cheese. Cover tightly with cling film and place in a freezer until ready to use.

6. To cook—thaw and bake in an oven preheated at 350 degrees for 30-40 minutes or until cheese is bubbly and brown.

Cheesy Greens Roll Ups

Prep Time: **40 minutes**

Servings: **9**

Ingredients:

9 lasagna noodles, cooked

2 cups spinach, chopped

2 1/2 cups ricotta cheese

1/2 cup grated Parmesan cheese

1 egg

A pinch of salt and fresh pepper

1 large jar of spaghetti sauce

9 tablespoons mozzarella cheese, shredded

Directions:
1. In a bowl, mix ricotta, parmesan spinach, egg and season with salt and pepper.
2. Spread mixture at the bottom of a baking dish.
3. Lay a lasagna noodle flat and divide spinach mixture evenly over it. Roll and place in the baking dish, seam side down. Repeat until you have gone through all the lasagna noodles.
4. Pour remaining sauce over the rolled pasta and top each roll with mozzarella.
5. Cover tightly with foil or cling film and place in a freezer.
6. Once ready to cook—thaw and bake in the oven for 40 minutes at 375 degrees.

Chicken, Ham And Cheese Casserole

Prep Time: **15 minutes**

Servings: **6**

Ingredients:

1 package chicken-flavored stuffing mix

1 (10 ounce) can condensed cream of chicken soup

1 tablespoon Dijon mustard

4 chicken breasts, skinned deboned and cooked; shredded

3 cups broccoli florets

2 cups ham, cooked and diced

6 slices Swiss cheese

Directions:
1. Combine all ingredients, except cheese slices, in a baking dish.
2. Top with cheese slices.
3. Cover tightly and place in a freezer until ready to cook.
4. To serve—thaw and bake in the oven for 40 minutes at 375 degrees.

Cheesy Ham And Potatoes

Prep Time: **15 minutes**

Servings: **8**

Ingredients:

1/2 cup onion, chopped

2 cups sour cream

1 (10 ounce) can condensed cream of chicken soup

2 cups Cheddar cheese, shredded

1 package hash brown potatoes

2 cups ham, chopped

Salt and pepper to taste

Directions:
1. Mix onions, sour cream, cheese, ham and soup in a bowl. Season with salt and pepper.
2. Arrange hash browns on a baking pan and pour sour cream mixture over it.
3. Cover tightly with foil and place in a freezer.
4. Once ready to cook—thaw and bake at 375 degrees for 40 minutes.

Make Ahead Mac And Cheese

Prep Time: **20 minutes**

Servings: **4-6**

Ingredients:

6 tablespoons butter

4 cups penne pasta, cooked

1/4 cup flour

5 cups milk

A pinch of salt and black pepper

4 cups Cheddar, grated

1 cup Parmesan, grated

1 cup buttery crackers, crushed

2 tablespoons parsley, chopped

Directions:
1. Melt butter in a saucepan and add flour while whisking.
2. Slowly add milk and season with salt and pepper. Allow mixture to boil and stir occasionally. Once mixture is thick, remove from heat and slowly add Cheddar and Parmesan.
3. Toss sauce with penne and mix well.
4. Transfer to a baking dish or individual ramekins, wrapping tightly with cling film. Place in the freezer.
5. Once ready to cook—thaw and bake in the oven for 20 minutes at 350 degrees.

Classic Pot Roast

Prep Time: 15 minutes

Servings: **4-6**

Ingredients:

1 3-pound roast

1 (12 ounce) cola-flavored soda

3/4 cup brown sugar

3/4 cup chili sauce

3/4 cup ketchup

3/4 pack dry onion soup mix

4-5 red potatoes

2 cups baby carrots

Directions:
1. Place all ingredients in a large freezer bag.
2. Shake bag up to allow ingredients to rub onto the meat and place in the freezer.
3. Once ready to cook—thaw and place in a slow cooker. Cook on low for 8-9 hours.

Chicken Parmigiana Bake

Prep Time: **25 minutes**

Servings: **4**

Ingredients:

4 chicken breasts, skinned and deboned

1 jar marinara sauce

2 cups mozzarella cheese, shredded

1 cup bread crumbs

2 tablespoons olive oil

1/2 cup assorted herbs—parsley, basil, oregano, cilantro

A pinch of salt and pepper

Directions:
1. Place chicken at the bottom of a baking pan.
2. Top with marinara sauce and mix with chicken.
3. Sprinkle cheese on top.
4. Combine bread crumbs with herbs and sprinkle on top of cheese.
5. Cover tightly with cling film and place in a freezer until ready to cook.
6. Once ready—thaw and bake in an oven for 25 minutes at 350 degrees.

Make Ahead Mongolian Beef

Prep Time: **20 minutes**

Servings: **4**

Ingredients:

2 teaspoons vegetable oil

1/2 teaspoon ginger, minced

1 tablespoon garlic, chopped

1/2 cup soy sauce

1/2 cup water

3/4 cup brown sugar

1 cup oil, for frying

1 pound flank steak, cut into strips

1/4 cup cornstarch

2 green onions, chopped

Directions:
1. To make the sauce—sauté ginger and garlic in oil and add soy sauce and water. Whisk in sugar and allow sauce to thicken. Remove from heat.
2. Meanwhile, dip beef into cornstarch and sauté beef in oil until brown.
3. Remove meat from oil using a slotted spoon and transfer to sauce mixture. Mix well.
4. Transfer mixture to a freezer bag and place in the freezer.
5. Once ready to cook—thaw and reheat in a saucepan. Serve over rice.

Breakfast Burritos

Prep Time: **35 minutes**

Servings: **24**

Ingredients:

24 flour tortilla wrappers

1 pound maple sausage

1 can black beans

1 large jar of salsa

8 eggs, lightly beaten

Italian seasoning, to taste

Cajun spice, to taste

1 small bag of potatoes, peeled and boiled

Directions:
1. Brown sausages in a skillet and add beans, eggs and salsa. Stir until eggs are firm.
2. Mash potatoes into the mixture and season with prepared seasonings. Mix thoroughly.
3. Spoon mixture into a tortilla wrapper and roll. Arrange on a baking dish, seam side down.
4. Place baking dish in a freezer, wrapped tightly in cling film.
5. Once ready to cook—thaw and microwave for 2-3 minutes.

Beef And Mushrooms

Prep Time: **15 minutes**

Servings: **4-6**

Ingredients:

3 pounds stew meat, cut into large cubes

1 (10 ounce) can cream of mushroom soup

4 cups mushrooms

1/2 cup apple juice

1 ounce onion soup mix

Directions:
1. Mix all ingredients in a large freezer bag. Shake well to incorporate all ingredients.
2. Place in a freezer until ready to cook.
3. Once ready—thaw and transfer contents to a crockpot. Cook on low for 10 hours.

All-American Casserole

Prep Time: **50 minutes**

Servings: **4-6**

Ingredients:

2 cups penne pasta, cooked

2 teaspoons of olive oil

1 onion, finely chopped

1 garlic clove, finely chopped

1 pound ground beef

3/4 teaspoon salt

1/2 teaspoon black pepper

4 cups diced tomatoes

2 tablespoons Dijon Mustard

2 cups Cheddar cheese, shredded

2 tablespoons tomato paste

Directions:
1. Sauté onions until tender and add garlic. Add beef and cook until browned. Season with salt and pepper.
2. Add diced tomatoes and mustard. Allow mixture to simmer and add additional salt and pepper if needed.
3. Place noodles in a greased baking dish and pour sauce over it.
4. Top with cheese. Cover tightly with cling film and foil.
5. Once ready to cook—thaw and bake for 20 minutes in an oven set to 375 degrees.

Veggie And Mozzarella Farfalle

Prep Time: **25 minutes**

Servings: **4**

Ingredients:

12 ounces farfalle pasta, cooked

1 pound broccoli florets, steamed and roughly chopped

3 large ripe tomatoes, chopped

3/4 pound onion, diced

4 garlic cloves, very finely minced

1 can chickpeas

3/4 cup basil, chopped

1/2 pound fresh full-fat mozzarella, divided

3 eggs, lightly beaten

1 cup cottage cheese

1 lemon, juiced

3/4 cup Parmesan, grated

2 teaspoons salt

1 teaspoon black pepper

Directions:
1. Toss pasta with tomatoes, broccoli, onions and garlic with chickpeas. Mix well.
2. Add basil and mozzarella.
3. Whisk eggs and cottage cheese and lemon juice together. Pour mixture into pasta and mix thoroughly.

4. Transfer mixture into a baking dish and sprinkle parmesan cheese on top. Wrap tightly with cling film and place in the freezer.
5. Once ready to cook—thaw and bake for 35 minutes in the oven set at 375 degrees.

Homemade Frozen Pizza

Prep Time: **25 minutes**

Servings: **8**

Ingredients:

1 18" pizza dough

1 cup tomato sauce

1/2 cup white onions

1/3 cup cilantro, chopped

1/3 cup mushrooms, sautéed

1/3 cup pepperoni, cooked

1/2 cup bacon, crumbled

2 cups Monterey Jack cheddar, shredded

1 cup mozzarella, shredded

Directions:
1. Take a rolling pin and flatten the pre-made pizza dough.
2. Spread tomato sauce onto the dough.
3. Sprinkle vegetables and herbs on top.
4. Finish off by evenly sprinkling cheese.
5. Wrap tightly with cling film and aluminum foil and place in the freezer.
6. Once ready—thaw and place in a preheated oven set at 475 for 15-20 minutes.

Easy Bake Chicken Pot Pie

Prep Time: **45 minutes**

Servings: **6**

Ingredients:

6 chicken breasts, cooked and shredded

4 potatoes, peeled and diced

2 cups carrots, cubed

1 cup butter

1 cup flour

2 1/2 teaspoons salt

1 teaspoon dried thyme

1 teaspoon pepper

3 cups chicken broth

1 1/2 cups milk

1 cup peas

1 can corn

4 pre-made pie crusts

Directions:
1. Sauté chicken with potatoes, carrots, peas and corn until cooked through.
2. In another pan, melt butter and add flour, salt, pepper and thyme. Slowly add chicken broth and milk. Allow mixture to simmer until thick and add chicken mixture.
3. Press bottom of pre-made pie crust onto a baking pan. Pour chicken mixture in and top with pie crust. Slice 4 slits onto the top and cover tightly with cling film.

4. Place in a freezer until ready to cook.
5. Once ready—thaw and bake in an oven for 70-80 minutes at 475 degrees.

Creamy Chicken With Salsa

Prep Time: **15 minutes**

Servings: **2**

Ingredients:

1 pound chicken breast

1 jar chunky salsa

1 (10 ounce) can cream of chicken soup

Directions:
1. Combine salsa, chicken soup and chicken in a freezer bag and seal.
2. Once ready to cook—place contents of plastic bag in a slow cooker and cook on low for 7 hours.

Baked Spaghetti

Prep Time: **30 minutes**

Servings: **4**

Ingredients:

1 (16 ounce) pack spaghetti noodles, cooked

1 pound ground beef

1 medium onion, chopped

1 (26 ounce) jar spaghetti sauce

1/2 teaspoon salt

2 eggs

1/3 cup Parmesan cheese, grated

5 tablespoons butter, melted

2 cups cottage cheese

4 cups mozzarella cheese, shredded

Directions:
1. Combine spaghetti sauce with beef and onions until cooked through over medium heat.
2. Whisk eggs, parmesan cheese and butter together.
3. Combine spaghetti noodles and egg mixture. Transfer to a baking dish and top with meat sauce, cottage cheese and mozzarella.
4. Cover tightly with cling film and freeze.
5. Once ready to bake—thaw and bake in an oven for 45 minutes.

Buttermilk Pancakes

Prep Time: **30 minutes**

Servings: **6**

Ingredients:

3/4 cup flour

3/4 cup almond flour

3 tablespoons sugar

1 1/2 teaspoons baking powder

1/2 teaspoon baking soda

1/2 teaspoon salt

1 1/2 cups buttermilk

1 tablespoon vegetable oil

1 large egg

1 large egg white

3/4 cup maple syrup

3 tablespoons butter

Directions:
1. Combine flour, sugar, baking powder, baking soda and salt in a bowl.
2. Meanwhile, whisk buttermilk, oil, egg and egg white together.
3. Combine both bowls together while stirring constantly.
4. Pour mixture into a freezer bag and seal.
5. Once ready to cook—thaw and ladle batter onto a skillet. Cook until brown on both sides.

Creamy Parmesan Chicken Penne

Prep Time: **40 minutes**

Servings: **2**

Ingredients:

6 tablespoons butter

A pinch of salt and pepper

6 cups penne, cooked

1 teaspoon olive oil

2 chicken breast halves, skinned and deboned and cooked

1/2 cup flour + 2 tablespoons

4 cloves of garlic, diced

6 cups of milk

2 cups mushrooms, trimmed and sliced thinly

1/2 cup sundried tomatoes, drained

1 1/2 cup Provolone, shredded

1 cup Parmesan, shredded

Directions:

1. Melt butter in a skillet and whisk in flour and garlic.
2. Slowly add milk and bring mixture to a slow simmer; add tomatoes and mushrooms.
3. Remove from heat and mix in Provolone.
4. Combine chicken and pasta in a baking dish and pour sauce over it.
5. Top with Parmesan cheese.
6. Wrap tightly with cling film and place in a freezer.

7. Once ready to cook—thaw and bake in the oven set at 350 degrees for 40 minutes.

Baked Pork Chops

Prep Time: **25 minutes**

Servings: **3**

Ingredients:

4 eggs

1 tablespoon Dijon mustard

1 tablespoon sage

8 pork chops, bone-in

2 cups bread crumbs

A pinch of salt and pepper

1/4 cup butter, melted

1/4 cup vegetable oil, for frying

Directions:
1. Combine all ingredients, except vegetable oil, in a freezer bag.
2. Place pork chops in the bag and allow to marinate. Place in a freezer until ready to cook.
3. Once ready to cook—thaw and fry in vegetable until cooked through.

Turkey Loaf

Prep Time: **15 minutes**

Servings: **3**

Ingredients:

1 tablespoon butter

2 cups onion, chopped

1 can mushrooms, sliced

3 garlic cloves, chopped

3/4 cup bread crumbs

1/4 cup chicken broth

3 tablespoons chopped fresh flat-leaf parsley

1 tablespoon low-sodium soy sauce

1 tablespoon Sriracha sauce

1 tablespoon Worcestershire sauce

1/2 teaspoon freshly ground black pepper

1 1/2 pounds ground turkey breast

1 large egg, lightly beaten

1/2 cup ketchup

1 tablespoon brown sugar

1/8 teaspoon dry mustard

1/8 teaspoon ground nutmeg

Directions:
1. Sauté mushroom and garlic in butter until tender.
2. Add bread crumbs, mushroom mixture and ground turkey in a bowl.

3. Whisk together ketchup, sugar, nutmeg and sugar in a bowl and mix in with turkey.
4. Place in a baking pan and wrap tightly with cling film. Place in a freezer.
5. Once ready to cook—thaw and bake for 40 minutes at 350 degrees.

Lemon Garlic Chicken

Prep Time: **15 minutes**

Servings: 6-8

Ingredients:

8 chicken breast halves, skinned and deboned

A pinch of salt and pepper

3 tablespoon olive oil

2 lemons, juiced

2 onions, chopped

4 clove garlic, minced

1 cup green olives, pitted and halved

2 cup chicken stock or reduced-sodium broth

1 teaspoon dried thyme

1/2 teaspoon crushed red pepper

Directions:
1. Combine all ingredients in a freezer bag and place in a freezer until ready to cook.
2. Once ready—thaw and empty contents into a slow cooker.
3. Cook on low for 6-7 hours.

Homemade Freezer Meal Recipes

1) Pork Tenderloin With Seasoned Rub

These juicy and spicy grilled tenderloins can be stored in the freezer for 3 months. For freezing purposes, season and char the tenderloins in a pan. When they cool down, seal them in foil wrap and place in a freezer bag. When ready to cook, thaw it in the refrigerator for 24 hours and grill according to the directions below.

Yield: 4

Cooking Time: **30 minutes**

List of Ingredients:

- Pork tenderloin, 1 ¼ pounds
- Garlic powder, 1 tsp.
- Salt, 1 tsp.
- Ground cumin, 1 tsp.
- Olive oil, 1 tbsp.
- Dried thyme, ½ tsp.
- Dried oregano, 1 tsp.
- Ground coriander, 1 tsp.

Procedure:

Preheat grill to medium high heat.

Combine all the dry spices together in a bowl. Drizzle oil and mix.

Rub the marinade all over the tenderloin using your hands.

Place the tenderloin on the grill and cook for 20 minutes. Turn occasionally to allow all the sides to cook well.

Before slicing allow it to sit for 5 minutes.

Serve.

2) Lasagna Rolls

These lasagna rolls are stuffed with spinach and tofu and cooked in spicy marinara sauce. This is one of the easiest recipes of lasagna and it can be stored in the freezer for up to 1 month.

Yield: 6

Cooking Time: **45 minutes**

List of Ingredients:
- Lasagna noodles, 12
- Garlic, 3 cloves, minced
- Salt. ¼ tsp.
- Tofu, 1 package of 14 oz. drained, rinsed and crumbled
- Marinara sauce, 1 jar of 25 oz.
- Spinach, 3 cups, chopped
- Mozzarella cheese, ½ cup, shredded
- Kalamata olives, 2 tbsp. Chopped
- Extra virgin olive oil, 1 tbsp.
- Parmesan cheese, ½ cup, shredded
- Crushed red pepper, ¼ tsp.

Procedure:

Prepare lasagna noodles according to package instructions. Keep aside in cold water covered.

Heat oil and sauté garlic until aromatic.

Add spinach and tofu and cook for 5 minutes. Stir occasionally. Transfer to a bowl and add red pepper, olives, 2/3 cup marinara sauce, salt and parmesan.

Add 1 cup marinara sauce in the pan.

Take each noodle and fill it with spinach and tofu mixture and roll. Place them in the pan over the sauce. Spread some sauce over the rolls.

Turn the flame high and cover the lid. Cook for a few minutes.

Turn the flame medium and cook for 5 minutes.

Top the rolls with mozzarella cheese and cook for 3 minutes with lid on. Serve.

3) Spaghetti And Meatballs In Tomato-Basil Sauce

This recipe makes a mighty meal for 8 people. The meatball mixture can be stored in the freezer for 2 weeks or more. Simply transfer the mixture in a Ziploc freezer bag and freeze. When ready to use just place it under running water for a minute and empty the mixture in a large dish. Cover it with plastic and microwave until well heated.

Yield: 8

Cooking Time: **25 minutes**

List of Ingredients:

For the Meatballs:

- Lean ground sirloin, 1 ½ pounds
- Garlic, 3 cloves, minced
- Onion, ½ cup, chopped
- Spaghetti, 12 oz.
- Black pepper, ¼ tsp.
- Parsley, ½ cup, chopped and divided

- Sweet Italian sausage, 6 oz. casting removed
- Salt, ½ tsp.
- Eggs, 2, beaten
- Bread, 2 sliced

For the Sauce:

- Dried basil, 1 ½ tsp.
- Black pepper, ¼ tsp.
- Unsalted crushed tomatoes, 2 cans of 15 oz.
- Salt, ½ tsp.
- Garlic, 5 cloves, minced
- Tomato paste, ¼ cup
- Sugar, 1 tbsp.
- Dry red wine, 1/3 cup
- Onion, 1 cup, chopped
- Olive oil, 1 tbsp.
- Unsalted diced tomatoes, 2 cans of 14.5 oz.

Procedure:

Preheat the oven to 450 F.

Heat oil in a Dutch oven and sauté onion with basil and garlic. Cook until tender and fragrant.

Add tomato paste and stir while cooking for 1 minute.

Add wine and cook for 2 minutes then add sugar and tomatoes and bring the mixture to a boil.

Then simmer on low flame for 25 minutes. Season with salt and pepper.

Now start preparing meatballs.

Grease 2 baking sheets and keep aside.

Make fine crumbs from the bread slices by processing it in the food processor.

Transfer crumbs in a large bowl. Add onions, eggs, garlic, parsley, sausages and beef. Season with salt and pepper.

Combine all the ingredients together and take spoonful of the mixture and roll it between your palms and make medium sized balls.

You will get around 40 meatballs.

Assemble meatballs on the prepared sheets and bake for 15 minutes.

When cooked, transfer the meatballs to the simmering tomato sauce and combine. Cook for another 10 minutes.

For immediate serving, prepare spaghetti according to the package directions. Combine meatball and sauce with spaghetti and top it with parsley.

Serve.

4) Vegetable Lover's Chicken Soup

This chicken soup recipe can be frozen for up to 3 months. It is healthy and very simple to make. It requires few ingredients which will most likely be already available in your kitchen. You can serve the bowl of soup with grated parmesan on top.

Yield: 2

Cooking Time: **35 minutes**

List of Ingredients:

- Chicken tenders, 8 oz. cut into chunks
- Baby spinach, 1 ½ cups, packed
- Salt, 1/8 tsp.
- Zucchini, 1 small, diced
- Plum tomatoes, 2, chopped
- Orzo/farfel line, 2 tbsp.
- Italian seasoning blend, ½ tsp.
- Chicken broth, 1 can of 14 oz.
- Shallot, 1 large, chopped
- Dry white wine, ¼ cup

- Extra-virgin olive oil, 1 tbsp.

Procedure:

Cook chicken in oil until golden brown. Transfer to paper towel to drain excess oil.

In the same pan add shallots and zucchini and season it with salt and Italian seasoning. Mix and cook until veggies are soft.

Stir chicken broth, wine, pasta and tomatoes. Bring to a boil on high flame.

Turn the flame low and simmer until pasta is tender.

Now add spinach and chicken tenders. Stir occasionally and cook for 2 minutes.

Serve immediately and refrigerate the remaining soup in a plastic bowl for up to 3 days.

5) Mini Chicken Burgers With Herbs

These mini burgers are perfect for a party or evening snacks. These can be kept in the freezer for 3 months. Follow all the directions through coating. Line a baking sheet with wax paper and place the uncooked coated patties on it and freeze them for 1 hour. Once they are set and frozen transfer in a large zip top freezer bag.

Yield: 8

Cooking Time: **25 minutes**

List of Ingredients:

- Ground chicken, 2 pounds
- Olive oil, 2 tbsp.
- Salt, 1 tsp.
- Parsley, ½ cup, chopped
- Dried bread crumbs, ½ cup
- Dried oregano, ½ tsp.
- Garlic, 1 ½ tsp., chopped
- Black pepper, ½ tsp.
- Lemon juice, 2 tbsp.

Procedure:

Combine chicken with lemon juice, garlic, parsley and oregano using a fork. Season with pepper and salt. Make 16 patties from the seasoned chicken.

Keep bread crumbs in a large bowl and coat patties evenly. Keep aside the coated patties.

Heat oil and fry patties until brown and cooked through.

Cover the lid and turn the flame low. Cook for 5-6 minutes.

You might want to work in batches.

Serve with hot-dog buns.

6) Baked Mac & Cheese

Who doesn't love mac and cheese? It is one of those meals that can make a person of any age group drool. This recipe of mac and cheese can be frozen for up to 3 months. Whenever hungry just take out the quantity you want to eat and thaw it and bake for 35 minutes or until bubbly.

Yield: 4

Cooking Time: **25 minutes**

List of Ingredients:

- Penne/elbow macaroni, 2 cups
- Dry breadcrumbs, 3 tbsp.
- Cottage cheese, 1 cup
- Ground pepper, to taste
- Paprika, ¼ tsp.
- All-purpose flour, 3 tbsp.
- Ground nutmeg, 1/8 tsp.
- Extra virgin olive oil, 1 tsp.
- Salt, ¼ tsp.
- Frozen spinach, 10 oz. package thawed

- Milk, 1 ¾ cup, divided
- Cheddar cheese, 2 cups, shredded

Procedure:

Preheat the oven to 450 F.

Grease an 8 inch baking dish and keep aside.

Combine breadcrumbs with paprika and mix. Drizzle oil and mix again.

Squeeze excess water from the spinach.

Heat 1 ½ cup milk until steaming. In a shallow bowl whisk flour in remaining milk and form a smooth mixture. Stir the flour mixture in the steaming milk and stir continuously until the white sauce starts to turn thick.

Remove the saucepan from stove and add cheddar cheese. Mix until well incorporated. Now add pepper, nutmeg, salt and cottage cheese. Mix again.

Cook pasta in boiling water until tender. Drain and rinse under cold running water.

Add pasta in the sauce and incorporate well.

Spread half of the macaroni in the greased dish evenly. Scatter spinach and top it with the remaining macaroni. Lastly top it with breadcrumbs and pop it in the oven.

Bake for 25-30 minutes or cover the dish and refrigerate for 2 days.

7) Turkey Tetrazzini

This creamy and rich turkey tetrazzini is a delicious pasta recipe. You can freeze it for up to 1 week. Cook the recipe according to the directions below but do not bake. Wrap the prepared casserole with plastic and freeze. When ready to cook, thaw it in the refrigerator for 2 hours and bake according to the directions.

Yield: 12

Cooking Time: **20 minutes**

List of Ingredients:
- Thin spaghetti, 1-½ pound
- Cream cheese, 1 block of 8 oz.
- Panko bread crumbs, 1 cup
- Turkey broth, 4 cups
- Fried bacon, 4 slices, cut into bits
- Salt, ½ tsp.
- Parmesan cheese, 1 cup, grated
- Butter, 4 tbsp.
- Black olives, 1 cup, chopped

- Extra broth, if required
- Green peas, 1-½ cups
- Flour, 1/3 cup
- Cooked turkey, 3 cups, diced
- Garlic, 4 cloves, minced
- White wine, 1 cup
- Monetary jack cheese, 1 cup, grated
- Pepper, to taste
- White mushrooms, 1 pound, quartered

Procedure:

Preheat the oven to 325 F.

Grease a casserole and keep aside.

Cook spaghetti according to the directions. Rinse under cold running water and keep aside.

Melt butter and sauté garlic until fragrant.

Add mushroom and salt. Stir fry until slightly browned.

Stir wine and cook until the wine reduces by half.

Now add flour and mix well in the mushrooms. Stir broth and cook until the mixture sets.

Turn the flame low and add cream cheese. Stir well to allow it to melt.

Now add turkey, bacon, olives, cheeses and peas. Season with salt and pepper. Cook for 2 minutes.

Transfer spaghetti to the mixture and incorporate well. Stir more broth is required. Your mixture should be a little soupy.

Transfer the mixture to the prepared casserole and top it with bread crumbs.

Bake for 20 minutes.

8) Blueberry Pumpkin Baked French Toast

Baked French toast can be kept in the freezer for up to a week. Simply perform all the steps including topping with berries and syrup. Cover and freeze. French toast requires thawing overnight in the fridge and may require more than 30 minutes to bake.

Yield: 8-10

Cooking Time: **35 minutes**

List of Ingredients:

- French baguette, 2 loaves, sliced into 24 pieces of 1 inch
- Blueberries, 3 cups
- Milk, 2 ½ cups
- Maple syrup, ¼ cup
- Pumpkin puree, ¾ cup
- Salt, ¼ tsp.
- Butter, ¼ cup
- Brown sugar, ¾ cup, firmly packed
- Ground cinnamon, 1 ½ tsp.
- Vanilla extract, 2 tsp.
- Eggs, 8

Procedure:

Preheat the oven to 375 F.

Grease a 9 x 13 pan.

Assemble baguette pieces on the prepared pan and keep aside.

Whisk eggs with brown sugar, salt, puree, milk, vanilla and cinnamon. Evenly coat the bread pieces in this mixture. Cover the pan and refrigerate overnight.

When ready to prepare, combine maple syrup with butter and microwave for a 1 minutes or two.

Top it with berries and pour the mixture over it.

Pop it in the oven and bake for 30 minutes.

9) Baked Beef Ravioli

Spicy layers of meat sauce and ravioli make for a perfect and easy meal. Beef ravioli can be kept in the freezer for up to a week. Follow all the directions below but do not bake. Wrap the casserole and freeze. When ready to cook thaw it for 48 hours in the refrigerator and bake according to the directions mentioned below.

Yield: 4-5

Cooking Time: **1 hour**

List of Ingredients:

- Ground beef, 1 pound
- Italian mix cheese, 2 cups, shredded
- Garlic, 3 cloves, minced
- Parmesan cheese, grated
- Pork sausage, ½ pound
- Mozzarella cheese, 2 cups, shredded
- Crushed Italian tomatoes, 1 can of 15 oz.
- Spaghetti sauce, 2 jars of 28 oz.

- Onion, ½, chopped
- Fresh cheese ravioli, 2 packages of 10 oz.

Procedure:

Preheat the oven to 375 F.

Grease a 9 x 13 casserole and keep aside.

Sauté onions until translucent.

Add garlic and cook until fragrant.

Add beef and sausages and cook until browned.

Remove excess fat from the pan and add tomatoes and sauce. Combine well.

Pour the sauce in to the prepared dish and spread out a thin layer.

Place a layer of cooked ravioli and add cheese. Repeat till the ravioli is all used. Last layer should be of the meat sauce.

Cover the casserole with foil and bake for 45 minutes.

Now remove foil and bake for 15 minutes.

Allow it to cool down for 10 minutes before slicing. Top it with parmesan cheese and serve.

10) Mocha Brownies

These heavenly rich brownies can be frozen for 3 to 4 days. These brownies are best enjoyed with chilled icing. You can double their richness by serving them with ice cream or topping them with hot fudge.

Yield: 20

Cooking Time: **45 minutes**

List of Ingredients:
- Unsweetened chocolate, 4 oz.
- Sugar, 2 cups
- All-purpose flour, 1-¼ cup
- Butter, 2 sticks
- Eggs, 4
- Vanilla extract, 3 tsp.

For the Icing:
- Cocoa powder, 1¼ cup
- Coffee, ½ cup, strongly brewed
- Butter, 2 sticks

- Vanilla, 3 tsp.
- Powdered sugar, 5 cups
- Salt, ¼ tsp.

Procedure:

Preheat the oven to 352 F.

Grease an 8 inch square pan.

Melt chocolate in the microwave and keep aside to cool.

Beat butter with sugar. Add eggs and beat on low speed. Gradually add melted chocolate and mix. Stir vanilla and mix.

Now gradually add flour and incorporate well.

Transfer the batter in the greased pan and spread evenly.

Bake for around 40 minutes.

Prepare the icing by combining butter with cocoa powder, vanilla, sugar and salt.

Stir coffee and beat until fluffy.

When the brownies cools down completely, slather it with the icing. You can make your icing as thick as you like.

Refrigerate until the icing if firm.

Slice the refrigerated brownies into squares and enjoy.

11) Pumpkin Chili

This extra hot pumpkin chili recipe can be stored in the freezer for up to 1 month. Store it in a zip top freezer bag. It requires overnight thawing time in the refrigerator. Transfer the contents in a large sauce pan and add some broth and heat.

Yield: 12

Cooking Time: **25 minutes**

List of Ingredients:
- Pumpkin puree, 1 can of 15 oz.
- Garbanzo beans, 1 can of 15 oz. drain and rinsed
- Dried oregano, ½ tsp.
- Garlic, 4 cloves, minced
- Paprika, ½ tsp.
- Black beans, 1 can of 15 oz. drained and rinsed
- Carrots, 3 large, diced
- Onion powder, ½ tsp.
- Pinto beans, 1 can of 15 oz. drained and rinsed
- Black pepper, 1 tsp.
- Onions, 2 large, diced

- Tomato paste, 2 tbsp.
- Garlic powder, ½ tsp.
- Bay leaf, 1
- Ground cumin, 1 tsp.
- Salt, 1 tsp.
- Crushed red pepper flakes, ½ tsp.
- Chili powder, 2 tbsp.
- Lentils, ½ cup any kind, rinsed
- Vegetable stock, 4 cups
- Tomatoes, 1 can of 28 oz. do not drain
- Olive oil, 2 tbsp.

Procedure:

Sauté onions and carrots with garlic in a Dutch oven for 5 minutes.

Season with salt and pepper.

Add all the ingredients and check seasoning. Bring the mixture to a boil while stirring constantly.

Now turn the flame low and simmer for 20 minutes. Stir occasionally.

Discard bay leaf and transfer to a serving bowl.

Top it with sour cream and serve.

12) Chipotle Chicken Chili

Spicy and flavorful chicken chili can be frozen for up to 1 week. Simply transfer the prepared chicken in a plastic bowl and refrigerate. Just before serving top it with cheese, cream and cilantro. This recipe compliments cornbread, Fritos or tacos.

Yield: 12

Cooking Time: 1 hour 15 minutes

List of Ingredients:
- Chicken breasts, 2 pounds, boneless, skinless and cubed
- Masa harina, ¼ cup
- Garlic, 4 cloves, minced
- Lime juice of 1 lime
- Onion, 1, diced
- Ground cumin, 1 tbsp.
- Good beer, 1 bottle of 12 oz.
- Olive oil, 2 tbsp.
- Tomatoes, 1 can of 14 oz.
- Chili powder, 1 tbsp.

- Salt, to taste
- Sour cream
- Pinto beans, 1 can of 14 oz. drained and rinsed
- Cheddar cheese, grated
- Lime wedges
- Black beans, 1 can of 14 oz., drained and rinsed
- Kidney beans, 1 can of 14 oz. drained and rinsed
- Cilantro
- Whole chipotle peppers in adobo sauce, 3, minced

Procedure:

Sauté onions with garlic in olive oil over medium flame.

Add chicken pieces and cook until browned.

Stir ¾ of the beer in the chicken and reduce the flame. Cook for 5 minutes.

Add beans, tomatoes and chipotle. Season with cumin, chili powder and salt.

Combine well and simmer for 1 hour. Cover the lid.

In a medium bowl mix remaining beer with masa harina and form paste.

Add this paste in the cooking mixture. Add lime juice and cook until thick.

Sprinkle cheese and cilantro. Serve sour cream.

13) Firecracker Asian Salmon

These salmon fillets can either be baked or grilled. Follow the directions below and freeze the marinated salmon fillets for up to 3 months. When ready to use, place it under cold running water for 1 or 2 minutes and bake or grill as you desire.

Yield: 8

Cooking Time: **20 minutes**

List of Ingredients:

- Soy sauce, 4 tbsp.
- Salmon fillets, 8
- Green onions, 4 tbsp., chopped
- Sesame oil, 1 tsp.
- Brown sugar, 3 tsp.
- Peanut oil, ½ cup
- Crushed red pepper flakes, 2 tsp.
- Red wine vinegar, 4 tbsp.
- Salt, ½ tsp.
- Ground ginger, 1 ½ tsp.

- Garlic, 2 cloves, minced

Procedure:

Preheat the oven to 400 F.

Combine all the ingredients except salmon in a large zip top freezer bag. Seal and shake well.

Add salmon and seal again. Shake lightly to coat the fillets in the marinade well.

Refrigerate for 1 hour.

Transfer the fillets and its marinade on a prepared baking dish and bake for 20 minutes.

14) Whole Wheat Pumpkin Pancakes

Pancakes are a regular breakfast item in any American family. Save yourself from the hassle of making pancakes every morning. You can prepare these pancakes a week ahead and freeze them. When ready to eat, just place them in a toaster and later microwave until well heated.

Yield: 12 pancakes

Cooking Time: **15 minutes**

List of Ingredients:
- Whole wheat flour, 2 cups
- Pumpkin puree, ½ cup
- Baking powder, 4 tsp.
- Eggs, 2
- Vanilla, 1 tsp.
- Cinnamon, 1 tsp.
- Butter, 4 tsp., melted
- Nutmeg, 1 pinch
- Milk, 2 cups

- Salt, ¼ tsp.
- Brown sugar, 2 tbsp.

Procedure:

Combine flour with sugar, cinnamon, baking powder, nutmeg and salt.

In another bowl whisk eggs with vanilla, butter, puree and milk.

Gradually add the flour with the egg mixture and combine well.

Let the batter stand for 5 minutes.

Grease a nonstick skillet with butter and pour spoonful of the batter. Spread out in a circle. Cook each side until browned.

Serve warm with maple syrup.

15) Slow Cooker Marinara Sauce

This hot marinara sauce will last you for months. Keep it in jars and seal tightly. Many dishes require marinara sauce for added flavor and hotness. So you can have this sauce ready to go whenever required.

Yield: 1 jar

Cooking Time: **4 hours**

List of Ingredients:

- Crushed tomatoes, 4 cans of 28 oz.
- Red pepper flakes, ½ tsp.
- Onions, 2 large, diced
- Parsley, 3 tbsp., chopped
- Water, 1 cup
- Garlic, 1 tbsp., chopped
- Olive oil, ¼ cup
- Salt, 1 tbsp.
- Dried basil, 1/3 cup, chopped

Procedure:

Heat oil and sauté onions with garlic until soft and fragrant.

In a 5 quart slow cooker, add the remaining ingredients and onion. Cover the lid and cook on low for 4 hours or more.

Store in mason jars and freeze.

16) Stuffed Poblano Peppers

These stuffed poblano peppers can be kept in the freezer for up to 2 months. Cover the dish with foil and freeze. When ready to use simply replace the foil with plastic wrap and microwave until heated.

Yield: 8

Cooking Time: 25 minutes

List of Ingredients:
- Poblano peppers, 8 large
- Dried ancho chilies, 4
- Ground cumin, 1 tbsp.
- Garlic, 10 cloves minced
- Cilantro leaves, ¼ cup

- Onion, 3 cups, chopped
- Queso fresco, 6 oz. crumbled
- Kosher salt, 1 tsp.
- Cream cheese, 4 oz. softened
- Black pepper, 1 tsp.
- Sugar, 2 tsp.
- Lime juice, ¼ cup
- Brown rice, 1 ½ cups, cooked
- Canola oil, 2 tbsp.
- Unsalted diced tomatoes, 2 cans of 14.5 oz.
- Lean ground sirloin, 12 oz.

Procedure:

Preheat your boiler.

Line a baking sheet with foil and assemble the peppers on it.

Broil until blackened and turn after every 6 minutes.

Transfer charred peppers in a paper bag and fold tightly. Keep aside for 15 minutes.

When the poblano peppers cool down, slit it and peel it and remove membranes and seeds. Keep aside.

Boil water and place ancho chilies and cover the bowl. Let it sit for 10 minutes then strain.

Turn the boiler temperature to 400.

Sauté onions with garlic in a nonstick skillet until tender and crisp. Transfer ½ of the onions on paper towel and leave the remaining in the pan.

Add beef in the remaining onions and season with salt and pepper. Cook until beef is done. Use a spoon to crumble it. Remove pan from flame.

Now add cream cheese and combine well.

Add rice and half quesco fresco. Incorporate well.

Process ancho chilies with lime juice, salt, cumin, sugar, onion mixture and tomatoes. Form a smooth mixture.

Grease 2 ceramic dishes and spread 1 cup sauce in each dish.

Stuff each poblano pepper with beef mixture and place in the prepared ceramic dishes.

Bake for 20 minutes.

Sprinkle with cilantro leaves.

17) Homemade Pizza Sauce

This homemade pizza sauce is so hot and flavorful that you will forget store bought sauce for a while. This recipe makes enough to fill up a jar and whenever you are craving for some pizza just slather it on the frozen dough and top it with veggies, chicken, cheese and bake. It is a long lasting sauce and can be refrigerated for 2 months.

Yield: 6 cups

Cooking Time: **30 minutes**

List of Ingredients:

- Chicken broth, ½ cup
- Dried oregano, 1 tsp.
- Garlic, 3 cloves, minced
- Fresh basil leaves, 10, chopped
- Sugar, 1 pinch
- Olive oil, 2 tbsp.
- Salt, to taste
- Black pepper, to taste
- Crushed tomatoes, 3 cans of 15 oz.

- Onion, 1 medium, chopped

Procedure:

Heat olive oil and sauté onions and garlic until onions are soft.

Stir broth and stir constantly until the mixture reduces by half.

Add tomatoes and season with salt, sugar, basil, pepper and oregano. Combine well.

Turn the flame low and simmer for 30 minutes or until thick.

18) White Chicken Pizza

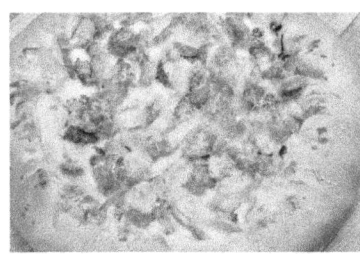

These individual pizza bites can be stored for up to 2 months in the freezer. Place the pizza on the stone and bake for 5 minutes and stack on a large dish and cover with foil. Whenever you wish to eat them simply place on a baking tray and preheat the oven to 450 F and bake until the cheese turns brown and bubbly.

Yield: 12

Cooking Time: **30 minutes**

List of Ingredients:

- Refrigerated fresh pizza dough, 30 oz. divided
- Greek yogurt, 1 cup
- Fresh basil, ¼ cup, chopped
- Thyme sprigs, 4
- Crushed red pepper, 1 tsp.
- Black pepper, 1 ½ tsp.
- Milk, 4 cup
- Cider vinegar, 4 tsp.
- Garlic, 8 cloves, crushed
- Olive oil, ½ cup

- Kosher salt, ½ tsp.
- Cooked chicken breast, 12 oz. shredded
- Thyme leaves, 2 tbsp.
- Italian blend cheese, 1 2/3 cups
- Fresh basil leaves, ½ cup
- Mozzarella cheese, 3 oz. break into small pieces

Procedure:

Preheat the oven to 450 F. place a pizza stone in the oven while it preheats.

While the oven is preheating allow the dough to rest at room temperature.

Heat oil in a pan and add thyme sprigs, red pepper, garlic and basil. Sauté until garlic becomes fragrant and brown. Remove from stove and allow to sit for 5 minutes.

Strain the contents and dispose of the solid particles.

Microwave milk with yogurt and vinegar for 6 minutes.

Use a sieve to obtain tiny curds from the mixture. Dispose of the liquid and mix curd with oil mixture and season with salt.

Make 12 portions from the dough and roll each portion between your palms to form a ball.

Place the dough balls on floured counter and flatten each dough gently forming a circle.

Grease each dough lightly with oil. Now top each piece with chicken, Italian blend cheese and mozzarella. Sprinkle black pepper and thyme leaves.

Take out the pizza stone from the oven and place a few pieces on it and bake for 8 minutes. You will have to do it in batches.

Sprinkle basil leaves and serve.

19) Homemade Freezer Jam

This sweet strawberry jam is free from any preservatives and artificial coloring. It is 100% healthy and easy to make. The jam can be stored in the freezer for 1 month.

Yield: 5 pints

Cooking Time: **25 minutes**

List of Ingredients:

- Strawberries, 2 cups
- Water, ¾ cup
- Sugar, 4 cups
- Dry pectin, 1 package of 1.75 oz.

Procedure:

Mash strawberries using a masher,

Add sugar and keep aside for 10 minutes.

Combine pectin in water and bring to a boil for 1 minute.

Add the water in the strawberries and let it sit for 3 minutes.

Transfer in air tight glass jar and cover tightly. Keep it on room temperature for 24 hours then keep in the freezer.

20) White Bean, Sage, And Sausage Soup

This healthy and nutritious soup can be kept in the freezer for up to 2 months. It's a delicious remedy for cold. Store the soup in a Ziploc freezer bag. When ready to use, heat in the microwave until pliable then transfer into a Dutch oven and heat for 20 minutes with lid on top.

Yield: 8

Cooking Time: **15 minutes**

List of Ingredients:
- Hot Italian sausage links, 20 oz. castings removed
- Dry white wine, 1 cup
- Onion, 2 cups, chopped
- Cannellini beans, 4 cans of 15.5 oz. rinsed and drained
- Garlic, 8 cloves, minced
- Fennel bulb, 1 cup, chopped
- Parsley, ¼ cup, chopped
- Crushed red pepper, 1 tsp.
- Tomato paste, 1 tbsp.

- Plum tomato, 2 cups, chopped
- Fresh sage, ¼ cup, chopped
- Unsalted chicken stock, 6 cups

Procedure:

Grease a Dutch oven with cooking spray and sauté onions, fennel bulb, garlic, sausages and red pepper. Cook until fragrant.

Turn the flame low and cook until sausages are browned and vegetables are soft. Use a spoon to crumble the sausages.

Add tomato paste and sage. Cook for 1 minute.

Stir wine and cook for 2 minutes.

Stir chicken stock and bring the mixture to a boil.

Turn the flame low and simmer for 6 minutes.

Now add beans and tomato and cook for another 3 minutes.

Top it with parsley and serve hot.

21) Honey-Garlic Chicken Kabob Marinade

This marinade recipe can be stored in the freezer for up to 2 weeks. The good thing about marinade is that the longer you keep it on meat the better it will taste. For your convenience you can place chicken and veggies on individual skewers because some veggies takes less time to cook than chicken and you do not want to overcook or burn your veggies.

Yield: 4

Cooking Time: **15 minutes**

List of Ingredients:

- Soy sauce, 1/3 cup
- Honey, 1/3 cup
- Extra virgin olive oil, ¼ cup
- Garlic, 2 cloves, minced
- Tomatoes, 2, diced
- Onion, 1, diced
- Bell pepper, 1 ½, diced
- Ground black pepper, ¼ tsp.

- Chicken breasts, 1 pound, cubed

Procedure:

Preheat the grill to 400 F.

Combine all the ingredients together in a bowl except for chicken and veggies. Mix well and let the marinade stand in the fridge for 10 minutes.

Add chicken and veggies in the marinade and refrigerate for 2 hours.

Assemble chicken and veggies on skewers and grill for 15 minutes.

Serve.

22) Broccoli-Cheese Chowder

The creamy and cheesy chowder can be kept in the freezer for up to 2 months. Perform all the steps except for adding cream and cheese. Transfer the mixture in a Ziploc freezer bag. When you want to eat, thaw it in the microwave until pliable. Transfer in the Dutch oven and add sour cream and cheese.

Yield: 6

Cooking Time: **45 minutes**

List of Ingredients:

- Broccoli crowns, 8 oz. cut into 1 inch pieces, stems and florets separated
- Celery, 2 stalks, diced
- Cayenne pepper, 1/8 tsp.
- Onion, 1, chopped
- Dry mustard, ½ tsp.
- Salt, 1/8 tsp.
- All-purpose flour, 1 tbsp.
- Extra-virgin olive oil, 1 tbsp.

- Garlic, 2 cloves, minced
- Cheddar cheese, 1 cup
- Carrots, 1 large, diced
- Potato, 1 large, peeled and diced
- Sour cream, ½ cup
- Vegetable broth, 2 cans of 14 oz.

Procedure:

Stir fry carrots, onion and celery in a Dutch oven for 5 minutes.

Add garlic and potato and cook until fragrant.

Add flour and mix. Add cayenne and cook for 2 minutes.

Stir broth with broccoli stems and bring the mixture to a boil.

Cover the lid and reduce the flame and allow it to simmer for 10 minutes.

Add florets and cover again, simmering for another 10 minutes.

Mash the chowder and add sour cream and cheddar in the Dutch oven. Cook for 2 minutes and season with salt.

Serve.

23) Roasted Lemon-Garlic Chicken With Veggies

This spicy and citrusy recipe can be stored in the freezer for 2 weeks. Prepare the marinade in the same way directed below and transfer it in a zip top freezer bag. Add chicken and veggies and seal the bag. Whenever you wish to eat it just thaw it in the fridge for 12 hours and bake according to the directions below.

Yield: 4

Cooking Time: **20 minutes**

List of Ingredients:
- Chicken breasts, 2 ½ breasts
- Garlic, 4 cloves, minced
- Sweet potato, 1 small, diced
- Lemon juice of 1 lemon
- Carrots, 3 large, diced
- Black pepper, ½ tsp.
- Salt, 1 tsp.

- Red potatoes, 2 medium, diced
- Dried parsley, ¼ tsp., crushed
- Olive oil, 6 tbsp.
- Green beans, ½ pound, trimmed

Procedure:

Preheat the oven to 425 F.

Combine green beans with carrots and potatoes. Season with lime juice, parsley, oil, salt, garlic and pepper. Toss the veggies well.

Grease a baking sheet and transfer the veggies in it. Cover it with plastic and refrigerate.

Transfer the remaining marinade in a zip top plastic bag and add chicken. Combine well by shaking. Refrigerate it for 1 hour or as many hours as you like.

When ready to cook, place the chicken on the veggies and bake for 40 minutes.

Serve.

24) Mini Mushroom And Sausage Quiches

These mini quiches are perfect for your upcoming cocktail party. Make these in bulk and freeze up to 1 month. However these quiches need to be stored individually in plastic wrap. When ready to eat, take out of the wrap and microwave for 60 seconds.

Yield: 1 dozen

Cooking Time: **30 minutes**

List of Ingredients:

- Turkey breakfast sausages, 8 oz. casting removed and crumbled
- Milk, 1 cup
- Scallions, ¼ cup, sliced
- Swiss cheese, ¼ cup
- Egg whites, 3
- Mushrooms, 8 oz. sliced
- Ground black pepper, ¼ cup
- Eggs, 5

- Extra virgin olive oil, 1 tsp.

Procedure:

Preheat the oven to 325 F.

Grease a muffin tin and keep aside.

Cook sausages in a large skillet until browned. Transfer to a plate.

Stir fry mushrooms until soft and browned. Add with sausages.

Now add cheese and scallions and season with black pepper.

Beat eggs and egg whites with milk and pour the mixture equally in the prepared muffin tray followed by spoonful of sausage mixture.

Bake for 25 minutes. Let it cool slightly before flipping it out of the muffin cups.

Serve.

25) Curried Corn Bisque

This is a very light recipe with few ingredients. The flavors are enhanced using hot sauce, curry powder and coconut milk. The bisque can be stored in the freezer for 2 months or you can refrigerate it for 2 days.

Yield: 8

Cooking Time: **25 minutes**

List of Ingredients:
- Onions, 1 cup, chopped
- Chicken broth, 2 cups
- Curry powder, 1 tbsp.
- Coconut milk, 1 cup
- Salt, ¼ tsp.
- Water, 2 cups
- Hot sauce, ½ tsp.
- Canola oil, 2 tsp.
- Frozen corn, 2 packages of 16 oz.
- Pepper, ¼ tsp.

Procedure:

Heat oil and sauté onions until translucent.

Season with hot sauce, curry powder, pepper and salt. Mix well.

Add broth, corn and water. Turn the flame high and bring to a boil.

Transfer the mixture in a food processor and puree it.

Transfer the soup in a saucepan and stir coconut milk. Cook until heated well.

Serve.

26) Iberian-Style Sausage & Chicken Ragù

The juicy and flavorsome chicken Ragu can be stored in the freezer for up to 3 months. Simply transfer the Ragu to an air tight container and microwave it on high whenever you wish you eat it.

Yield: 8 cups

Cooking Time: **1 hour**

List of Ingredients:

- Linguisa (Portuguese style sausage), 8 oz. diced
- White wine, 3 cups
- Chicken broth, 2 cups
- Garlic, 2 tbsp., chopped
- Saffron threads, 1 pinch
- Pimento de la Vera, 2 tbsp.
- Ground pepper, to taste
- Tomatoes, 4 cups, diced and seeded
- Chicken thighs, 2 pound, boneless and skinless, cut into chunks
- Parsley, ¼ cup, chopped

- Onion, 3 cups, chopped
- Extra virgin olive oil, 1 tbsp.
- Salt, ½ tsp.

Procedure:

Stir fry sausages until browned.

Add garlic and onion. Cook for 10 minutes.

Add pimento de la Vera and coat well. Cook for 1 minute.

Now add chicken and season with pepper and salt. Cook for 5 minutes while stirring constantly.

Stir wine and turn the flame high. Cook for 8 minutes. By this time wine had been reduced by a third.

Stir broth followed by tomatoes, saffron and parsley. Turn the flame low and simmer for 1 hour or more until chicken is cooked through. Serve.

27) Sausage Gumbo

Cajun seasoning is the key ingredient of this recipe. This seasoning is a blend of various spices like cayenne, paprika, pepper, garlic, onion powder etc. This recipe can be stored in the freezer for up to 3 months or refrigerated for 3 days. Store it in a zip top freezer bag.

Yield: 8

Cooking Time: **40 minutes**

List of Ingredients:
- Hot Italian turkey sausage links, 12 oz. castings removed
- Chicken broth, 4 cups
- Garlic, 4 cloves, minced
- Scallions, 1 bunch trimmed and sliced
- Onion, 1 large, chopped
- Tomatoes, 4 cups, chopped
- All-purpose flour, 2 tbsp.
- Instant brown rice, ¾ cup

- Cajun seasoning, 1 tsp.
- Okra, 2 ½ cups, chopped
- Canola oil, 2 tsp.

Procedure:

Heat a medium Dutch oven and cook sausages for 5 minutes. Use a wooden spoon to crumble it. Transfer to paper towel and keep aside.

Add oil and sauté onion until soft. Add Cajun seasoning and garlic. Cook until aromatic.

Now add flour and mix for 1 minute. Add tomatoes and cook for 2 minutes. Stir occasionally.

Add chicken broth and cover the lid. Turn the flame high and boil the mixture.

Now add rice, sausages and okra and mix. Turn the flame low and simmer for 12 minutes.

Dish out and serve with scallions.

28) Jamaican Beef Patties

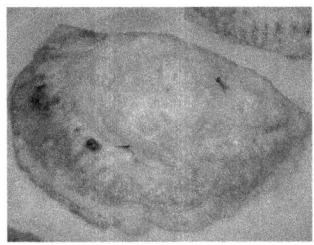

These beef stuffed patties are spicy and crunchy. They make for a perfect evening snack and compliment tea very well. These patties can be kept in the freezer for up to 6 months. Follow all the steps except for the baking part and wrap the unbaked patties tightly. When ready to eat simply keep them at room temperature for a few minutes then bake for 40 minutes on 400 F.

Yield: 6

Cooking Time: **45 minutes**

List of Ingredients:

- All-purpose flour, 1 ¼ cups
- Cold unsalted butter, 4 tbsp.
- Egg yolk, 1
- Baking powder, ¼ tsp.
- Ice water, 1/3 cup
- Ground turmeric, 1 tsp.
- Whole-wheat pastry flour, 1 cup
- Salt, ¾ tsp.

- Canola oil, 5 tbsp.

For the Filling:
- Lean ground beef, 8 oz.
- Dried thyme, ¼ tsp.
- Salt, ¼ tsp.
- Scallions, 1 bunch, minced
- Water, ¼ cup
- Ground turmeric, ¼ tsp.
- Scotch bonnet chili pepper, 1 tsp.
- Breadcrumbs, ¼ cup

Procedure:

For crust, combine flour with turmeric, whole wheat flour, baking powder and salt.

Slice butter into chunks and add in the flour mixture. Use your fingers and rub them until small in size.

Drizzle oil and use a fork to mix.

Combine water with egg yolk and whip.

Stir the egg mixture in the flour bowl and incorporate everything well. Knead into fine dough. Wrap the bowl with plastic and place in the refrigerator for 1 hour.

To make filling, cook beef with chili pepper and scallions. Use a spoon to crumble beef. Cook for 8 minutes.

Add breadcrumbs, turmeric, water, salt and thyme. Combine well.

Preheat the oven to 400 F.

Make 6 equal portions of the dough and roll each piece into a round shape. Use a bowl to even out the sides.

Place ¼ cup filling on one side of the flatten dough and cover it with other side making a semi- circle. Use a fork to seal the edges.

Assemble the patties on a baking tray and bake for 40 minutes.

29) Squash, Chickpea & Red Lentil Stew

This healthy and complete vegan stew is a delicious and filling meal. Follow all the steps and transfer the prepared stew in a zip top freezer bag and store in the freezer for up to 1 month. This stew can also be refrigerated for 3 days.

Yield: 8

Cooking Time: **6 hours**

List of Ingredients:
- Dried chickpeas, ¾ cup
- Ground cumin, 1 ½ tsp.
- Onion, 1 large, chopped
- Kabocha squash/butternut squash, 2 ½ pounds, peeled and seeded, cut into cubes
- Roasted unsalted peanuts, ½ cup
- Red lentils, 1 cup
- Salt, 1 tsp.
- Tomato paste, 2 tbsp.
- Carrots, 2 large, peeled and cut into ½ inch pieces

- Ginger, 1 tbsp., peeled and minced
- Lime juice, ¼ cup
- Saffron, ¼ tsp.
- Vegetable broth, 4 cups
- Ground black pepper, ¼ tsp.
- Cilantro leaves, ¼ cup, chopped

Procedure:

Soak chickpeas in cold water overnight. Keep them covered.

Next day mix chickpeas with carrots, onion, squash, salt, broth, saffron, cumin, tomato paste, lentils, cumin, ginger and pepper.

Cook them in a slow cooker on low with lid on. Cook for 6 hours or until chickpeas are tender.

Lastly add lime juice and top with cilantro and peanuts.

30) Chile & Beer Braised Brisket

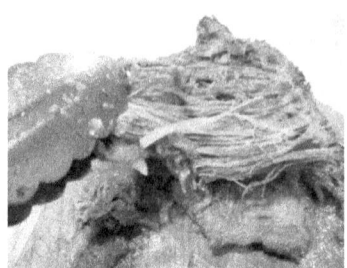

Braised in beer, these briskets take hours to bake. The simple way is to prepare it 3 days before the main day and freeze. You can also freeze it for up to 3 months. Whenever you wish to eat, microwave it and enjoy.

Yield: 6

Cooking Time: 30 minutes

List of Ingredients:

- Dried new Mexico/Anaheim, 6, stemmed and seeded
- Ground cumin, 2 tsp.
- Pinto beans, 1 can of 15 oz. rinsed
- Salt, 1 tsp.
- Onion, 1 large, coarsely chopped
- Trimmed flat, first cut brisket, 2 pounds
- Fire-roasted tomatoes, 1 can of 14 oz. diced
- Canola oil, 1 tbsp.
- Mexican lager, 1 cup
- Garlic, 4 cloves, chopped

- Chili powder, 1 tbsp. + 1 tsp.

Procedure:

Preheat the oven to 350 F.

Break chilies into pieces and keep in hot water for 20 minutes. Keep it covered. Drain.

Blend tomatoes with chilies, cumin, onion, salt, garlic and chili powder until smooth. Pour the mixture in a bowl and add beer.

Heat oil in a Dutch oven and cook brisket until browned from sides. Add the sauce and simmer on low flame.

Cover the Dutch oven and bake for 2 hours. Lastly add beans and bake for an additional 1 hour.

Once cooked, spoon out meat from the sauce and shred it. Place it back in the sauce and serve.

www.ingramcontent.com/pod-product-compliance
Lightning Source LLC
Chambersburg PA
CBHW071442070526
44578CB00001B/198